ORIENTAL TUNES

R. RAVIKUMAR

ISBN
Paperback 979-8-89233-895-0

To my wife, Sashi

This book is about Japan and China
Which is written in Japanese as
この本は日本と中┌についてです
And in Mandarin as
┌本┌是┌于日本和中┌的

CONTENTS

PREFACE

There are few things more universal than a person's love and comfort with one's country, city, and home. Home is, without doubt, sweet. However, living away from it, in different countries, can provide some memorable experiences and learnings and is certainly something to look for. It brings along lots of learning, surprises, challenges, humour, frustrations and fun. My family and I were fortunate to get this opportunity when we lived outside India for some years, in Singapore, Japan, and China – all Asian, but each one with a distinct culture and tradition.

Many Indians are widely travelled and well-read about other countries. But perhaps, most of the exposure is to the West – America and Europe in particular. Even if people have not lived there, they have a number of relatives and friends who give them a good account of these places. However, people's exposure to the East is comparatively limited. We know the big headlines of the culture and customs of say, Japan or China. We admire the Japanese for being very punctual and extremely quality-conscious. We often compare India with China in culture and population size and their economic success has caught our attention.

But knowledge is limited to a few headlines. Living there allowed me the opportunity to experience their culture and customs in greater detail, and so I thought it might be useful if I documented and shared it.

There are hundreds of books and online materials about these countries. So why another book? Why this one? Recognising the relevance of these questions, I have chosen to focus on personal anecdotes so that the nuances of society and behavioural aspects are brought out and will help provide the reader with a better understanding. I will discuss and provide examples of just how polite the Japanese are, what aspects of their culture make them produce such high-quality goods, what is the life of a foreigner in a country where there is no common language between them and the local people, and so on. To be of interest, my writing had to comprise lesser-known facts and information that would be new to the readers. So, about Japan and China, I will write about the society and culture of the country, sharing anecdotes and experiences of the family, and also my own thoughts on a few topics. The tone of the book will be about more positive aspects, and I will avoid dwelling on negative aspects of these countries. On some topics, I have chosen to draw from online material to present facts and ensure authenticity.

At the current pace at which the world moves, since the time we lived there, social changes must have occurred, although customs and traditions carry centuries of legacy and do not tend to change significantly over short periods of time. Post-Covid, there are several changes that have occurred in China, but I have opted to keep it outside the purview of this book. The nature of change in most countries these days is somewhat similar, with the impact of technology and social media, i.e., greater dissemination of information (good or bad, real or fake), wider communication networks, higher levels of individualism, a greater commonality in work culture, and so on. The two countries that I will speak about are no different. So, I thought that dwelling on them would not have much value.

When you live outside the home country, to enjoy the novelty that the host country has to offer, many things have to go well. In our case, it did, and the credit for it goes to my wife, Sashi, who made a living in foreign countries as comfortable as possible. Relocation involves a huge amount of work: searching for housing, the laborious work of packing and moving goods, being without a house and your personal belongings for a few weeks, twice - when leaving the country and entering another, researching children's education, and adapting to the changes in the new city. She bore the brunt of the changes, the hard work, and the research that goes with it. Our food habit is vegetarian, and in countries like Japan and China, she ensured that vegetarian food was on our plates every day. I have one complaint against her, though. That Sashi never made Sushi.

I wondered how I should categorise this book – as Memoirs or Travelogue or simply ramblings about countries. Perhaps it's a mix of them all. A friend of mine described the exercise of book writing as one of nervous energy. Based on my experience with this book, I interpret it as being the nervousness of a writer and the energy of nostalgia.

Hope you like the read.

Ramanan Ravikumar

ACKNOWLEDGEMENTS

I would like to thank people who helped me write this book. Balachandar and Sridhar, who lived in either country, shared useful feedback on draft material. Kavita, my niece, holds a world record for being the only South Indian to have never tasted the delicacy *Sambhar*. Bad Karma. Despite this drawback, thanks to her language and presentation skills, she helped edit material. My neighbours Masuko-san and Sani-san were kind enough to share their inputs on the recent changes in Japanese society. My sons Sujay and Sandeep helped with editing, design and creating a final product.

Japan

CHINA
RUSSIA
Hokkaido
Sapporo
NORTH
KOREA
Sea of Japan
Akita
Honshu
Sendai
SOUTH
KOREA
JAPAN
TOKYO
Nagoya
Yokohama
Hiroshima
Kobe
Kyoto
Kitakyushu
Osaka
Fukuoka
Shikoku
Kyushu
East
China
Sea
NORTH PACIFIC OCEAN
facts.co

Chapter 1

OUR STAY AND EXPERIENCES

We landed at Tokyo's Narita airport on a Friday evening. The airport is 70 km away from Tokyo city, and usually, a family of 4 would take a cab, but taxis are very expensive (between $150 - 200), and hence even business travellers use a bus ($15-20) to get to the city. Buses are frequent, comfortable, and can accommodate enough luggage. The famed Japanese politeness and culture of bowing to people were visible as we loaded baggage and boarded the bus. Each loader bowed to us both before taking the baggage trolley from us and after they finished loading. Even the loaders who were attending to other passengers bowed to us as they passed by us.

During bus rides, to avoid disturbance to fellow passengers, there is an unwritten rule that passengers talk softly among themselves and not use mobile phones. Despite the drive to the city that day being for a much longer time of two hours compared to the normal hour and 15 minutes, no one spoke on the phone. One cannot resist a comparison with the mobile phone habits of Indians. In trains and buses, we talk long and loud, conduct business negotiations, and these days even do video calls. In an aircraft, upon landing, the moment the air hostess announces permission to use phones, everyone frantically picks up the mobile and start calling the spouse (presumably their own), very keen to announce the safe landing of their 'shuttle'. We try to confirm that the Earth continued to rotate at the same speed when we were 'up in the air' and give detailed instructions to our car driver to pick us up quickly without wasting a second.

After arriving in the city, we checked into Tokyo's Okura hotel for a 2-week stay before moving into our apartment. A day later, I 'graciously' let my wife, commute 40 km to the American School in Japan (ASIJ), where my sons were to study, to show them the school and find out more about it. With two reluctant boys for company, she changed three trains to reach the school, finding her way in an alien city where no one even attempted to speak English.

House Selection

A month earlier, we had our first experience of apartment selection, and the process was interesting. As per company policy, I was allowed to travel with my spouse to do a look-see trip to Tokyo to finalise housing and schooling. In preparation for the house search, we had to fill out a form specifying our requirements and preferences. In Tokyo, we were introduced to two real-estate agents who shortlisted 15+ houses, and over a three-day period, they showed us around. The entire process was super-efficient. About each house, the agents came prepared with a document with lots of data:

Its exact location, size, and number of rooms.

The rent quoted and the owner's name.

Which of our requirements and preferences it met or did not meet.

A printed map of the neighbourhood.

Walking time to the nearest metro rail station.

Walking time to the school bus stop, approx. bus arrival time, and driving time to the school.

List of nearby shops/marketplace/restaurants appropriate to us, and so on.

Wow.

Two instances stand out in memory from the search. In one case, the apartment was exactly opposite my office. Upon reaching the place, when I realised this, I told the agent that I did not want to live so close to the office and prefer not to spend time seeing that apartment. I thought it was a practical approach to avoid seeing one, which I will definitely not select, but it appears it is not considered good manners in that country. The agent seemed a little upset. Once a landlord has been told that his/her house is on the list, it has to be visited. I asked, "Can we tell the landlord that we didn't opt for it," but that was not an acceptable practice, so we proceeded to see the apartment with all seriousness.

In another instance, the agent did not readily have a particular piece of information we asked for about an apartment and promised to revert. By the time we returned to our hotel about an hour later for lunch, the information was faxed by her office and waiting for us at the hotel reception.

Usually, in the selection of housing, proximity to schools is an important factor, but most international schools are situated far away from the city (30-40 km away) since they need, and get, access to a large piece of land. So, this factor did not go into our house selection.

As forewarned, language problems made settling down very challenging, having to deal with Japanese-speaking people to obtain basic necessities like a new landline phone, mobile, and internet connections.

Once our goods arrived from Singapore and the furniture was put in place, we started looking for luxuries – like Indian TV channels. The only available Indian channels in Japan then were Sahara TV – 10 of them in different Indian languages, some of which even carried news of important events like a mother-in-law and daughter-in-law fight. The other facility we wanted was one that would let us watch Cricket. Willow.tv's webcast answered our prayers, although the quality of the webcast we received was like the performance of the Indian team – somewhat blurred and erratic.

We lived in a suburb called Roppongi. It had two interesting contrasts. On the one hand, it is one of Tokyo's most opulent, upmarket areas, featuring world-class art museums, Michelin-starred restaurants, and several luxury shopping destinations. On the other hand, it is also one of Tokyo's raucous party neighbourhoods, full of restaurants, bars, and clubs that stay open late[1]. It had a couple of very popular 'red-light' streets. The main one was in the centre of the suburb, and one had to walk past it frequently. Past 9pm, These streets were lined up with prostitutes, many wobbling drunkards, and people lying on the road. Each evening around 7 pm, small palm-sized pamphlets would be plastered all through every footpath railing in those streets, providing information and contact details of prostitutes. Then, the next morning, the same staff who pasted the pamphlets would systematically remove each one of them.

This routine took place every single evening and morning without fail.

A *Shaky* Birthday Celebration

An early milestone in Tokyo was my wife Sashi's xxth birthday. The usual low-key celebration was marred by an earthquake – the first one that we would experience in Japan. The boys, who had never experienced one before in their lives, were a bit scared initially but also found it amusing to see so many things rattling in the house. During our two-year stay, there were many earthquakes – at least 20 of them. So common, in fact, that some of them barely got reported in the newspaper.

According to the Seismology Society of Japan, including the quakes too small for humans to feel, there are more than 100,000 earthquakes every year in Japan and surrounding areas. About 1% of them—1,000 to 1,500—exceed 1 on the seismic intensity (Richter) scale, meaning they are strong enough for people to notice[2]. Just recently, on January 1, 2024, quakes stuck the Ishikawa prefecture 155 times, killing 48 people. During the many quakes that occurred during office hours, work in the office proceeded rather normally without much panic, perhaps because it was so common, and there was no history of accidents, except during massive, disastrous quakes. A helmet was placed next to every desk in the office for ready use. All structures across the country are built to withstand quakes, and this safety feature gives added confidence. If one were at all to be part of an earthquake experience, Japan would be among the safer places to be in!

Schooling

My sons went to ASIJ - The American School in Japan, a quality international school that was established more than 100 years ago. The boys liked studying there. Teachers were highly qualified and had the experience of working in different countries. When my 12-year-old niece visited Tokyo on a holiday, the school even allowed her to attend a day's classes just for experience. As I read through the mathematics curriculum of grade 4, I observed that what was being taught in grade 4 had already been covered in grade 2 in India. As I churned this in my head, I was confused about which system is better – is the international system slow or, conversely, the Indian system too fast? Why do they teach in grade 2 in India/Asia what other countries seem to be comfortable waiting until grade 4? I still don't know what the right answer to that question is.

My sons did experience racial discrimination and ignorance—a good learning from global living. Some roughing-up is bound to do them good in the long run. Once when talking to a friend, my younger son said, "I spoke to my grandmother yesterday…". To this, his American classmate interjected and asked, "You have a grandmother? You are from India. In poor countries, people don't have grandmothers." Hmm, what a theory! A frequent question asked of them was, "In India do you move around on an elephant?". In another instance, his physical trainer, angry that my son's sacred thread/Janeu (a religious symbol) interfered with swimming, chided him, pulled it, and threw it away despite his pleas not to do so. It emotionally upset a 9-year-old who must have been confused between cultures. Back home from school, he narrated the incident. The following day, I called the teacher to discuss the incident and find out what happened. His immediate reaction was to deny any such act on his part. I told him that a nine-year-old child is more likely to speak the truth than an adult, and so something must have happened. He then tried to justify what he did. I warned him to be culturally more sensitive and to not repeat such behaviour. I also complained to the school authorities, who told me later that they had spoken with the teacher to be more culturally sensitive in the future.

The drive from home to school (40 km distance) by the school bus took an hour plus. The bus was a busy place. The role of bus monitor was assigned by rotation to the children, and the monitor was paid a fee for managing other students on the bus. My son earned Yen 11,000 and over the following few years spent 20x of that, each time citing his earnings as the source! During the bus ride, students did homework for other students.

At school, children of age 12 or 13 started having boyfriends and girlfriends. Slightly older ones displayed their affection publicly, engaging in kissing. My older son who was approaching his teens, may have been intrigued initially and, perhaps, wondering when his own turn would come ☺. But the younger one was too small and used to narrate stories to his mother. As Asian parents, my and my wife's reaction was predictable—very uncomfortable with the environment our children were being exposed to. But that, I suppose, is what international living is about.

There was another incident experienced by my older son, Sujay, during a history class in grade 9 (although it was in his Shanghai School, not Tokyo). The students were asked to write an essay about Hinduism. The subject was "How Hinduism had adversely impacted the growth of India." In the course of doing his homework, he mentioned it to us. My wife spent time understanding details on the exact nature of discussions on this topic in class and what was expected of students. It appeared to be around practices like Sati. She met his teacher to discuss, further understand, and clarify, if necessary. She shared information about India's culture/religion and suggested that what was being taught to the students by way of practices such as Sati was not a part of Hindu religious scriptures or teachings but was a social practice (that too practiced in only two states in the country – Rajasthan and Madhya Pradesh) and was perpetuated in the name of religion by its beneficiaries in society. The practice of using religion to get society to behave in a certain manner was, after all, common worldwide and exploited by people of all faiths. Once the teacher was convinced, in a subsequent class, she shared what she had heard with the students and admitted that she stood corrected on some of what was taught earlier. She was a highly educated and travelled history teacher, and it was indeed very gracious of her to acknowledge and revise what she was teaching.

Tamilese

In recent years, I'm told more young people know and are comfortable speaking in English, but back then, with the exception of a few Japanese people in offices, no one spoke English. So, when we commuted even within the city, we needed to carry printed addresses and area maps. Communication with the locals was mainly in sign language. The words required to make up a sentence were in English. After some time, I started speaking with the local Japanese in my mother tongue – Tamil. I thought that in any case, I mainly used sign language coupled with English words, which they didn't understand anyway. So, when using words as a filler to construct a sentence, what difference would it make to them whether I used English, Swahili, or Tamil?

For example, in a taxi, I would say - "Ki-iro sign kitte migi thirumbu": "Ki-iro (yellow in Japanese) kitte (near in Tamil), migi (right side in Japanese) thirumbu (Tamil word for turn)." After all, all that the cab driver needed to know was the Japanese words to turn right near a yellow signboard. I had to stop this practice because my young sons, rather amused by my antics, would start giggling, and I realised that the Japanese would not know what they were laughing about and would find it offending.

Our First Holiday and a Nightmare

Our first holiday was a 5-day trip to Hong Kong to visit my cousin. The holiday was a busy and enjoyable one. The families had a blast, especially since my cousin had two sons of the same age as mine. Since December was also IBM's annual financial closing, I returned to Tokyo a day earlier than the rest of the family.

What was to follow was a disaster that would be among my family's darkest days. After landing at the airport around midday, I went home, opened the door, kept the luggage near the entrance, and went away to work without entering the rooms in the apartment. At the end of the day's work, at around 8 pm, I went to a friend's place near my apartment for dinner. Then around 10 pm, I returned home and entered the house… I walked into the bedroom and realised…. that there was a burglary in our Tokyo apartment during our travel!! Burglars entered it and took away valuables. The locking system on our main door at home was rather easy to break. It was built that way to facilitate easy evacuation during earthquakes and, in general, the low levels of burglary in Japan and Tokyo. Once the burglars broke in, they walked straight into their 'target,' the master bedroom. When we moved from Singapore to Tokyo, we purchased a safe-deposit vault with a digital number lock to keep valuables, mostly gold jewelry and cash. We were among the very few who had a vault at home. It didn't help us. They ripped it open using a toolkit from our own home. We lost a lot of money. Everything in the house was untouched and intact, without any sign of such an event having taken place. The burglars, it appears, had inside information about our apartment. How else would they go straight to the locker in one of the rooms without touching any item in any cupboard or drawer in the house? We ended up being among the very small percentage of victims in that country. Later, we were told that burglaries did occur in Tokyo during Christmas time because most foreigners travelled out of the country on vacation, leaving their houses unguarded. Unfortunately, I had not taken insurance cover.

The family arrived from Hong Kong the next day, and I had the difficult task of breaking the news to them. I went to the hotel where airport buses drop passengers, about 5 mins from home. I had to break this news to them at the bus stop before they entered the house. It will not come to anyone as a surprise if I say that, now, many years later, their reaction remains vivid in my memory. They were totally shaken, and the children instantly started crying. It shook the family to think that rogue strangers had entered our home - and looted it. Fear entered our minds regarding our safety in Tokyo. It was not easy on the children, still only 12 and 9.

The building we lived in did not have any security personnel since it was too expensive to have one but it had CCTV cameras installed for security. I called the landlord and complained about the event. He didn't say anything. I asked him to look into how something like this could possibly have happened. He called back after a few hours to say that the police had seen the CCTV footage and did not find anything unusual during the days we were away travelling. It was a lie – either the police and the landlord didn't see the footage (because they reverted to us quickly, within just a few hours of our complaint) or they were clearly trying to cover up what they saw. When my wife told her European friend in our building, she asked us not to believe them and see the CCTV footage for ourselves. The landlord was reluctant to give us the tapes, but we insisted, thanks to our neighbour, who not only pushed us to view it but sat through the video viewing to give us moral support. Rather nice of a person we barely knew. As we viewed the video minute by minute, there was clear footage of masked men entering the building, breaching security with ease. There was no CCTV in my floor lobby, but it became clear as to what had happened. Viewing the video was an extremely disturbing experience.

We called the police and lodged a complaint with the nearby police station. Lodging a complaint with them was painful and, as it turned out, totally useless. They came home and took fingerprints of various items and ours. The only ones they could match with the locker were mine! They spent an hour filling out forms and repeatedly asked for pictures or drawings of each item lost. The police wanted pictures of jewelry. A day later, they called us to the police station. Here is the opening conversation:

Station-in-charge: "From our investigation, we have found an important piece of information."

Me: My hopes rise, "What is that?"

Station-in-charge: "The burglars are not Japanese."

Me: #^@$% (saying cuss words in my mind)

Oof, did the nationality of the burglars even matter to us?

He then added that the thieves were foreigners. We asked them the basis of this finding since the video showed them entering the building wearing a mask which covered their faces. The police had no answers. So it was a case of pride and prejudice. National pride that thieves could not be Japanese.

At the police station, when they wanted to know what type of jewels were lost, we showed my wife's Mangalsutra (a necklace worn by a Hindu woman upon marriage) as an example. They asked her to remove it so that they could measure it and brought a flat plastic foot-ruler. You can imagine her reaction when asked to remove her Mangalsutra. Fume! When we said that we lost cash, they asked whether the cash belonged to me or my wife? Just how much more ridiculous could they get. Do husbands and wives tag their cash separately at home as his and hers? How did it matter whose cash it was? When we were ready to leave the station, we asked them the chances of finding the culprits. The officer said that that particular police station had a bad record of catching burglars and chances of finding the culprits are low (he actually said that). True enough, in the following months, we never heard back from the police. Based on this entire experience, my respect for Indian policemen increased. They do a far better job, particularly if we factor in that they are understaffed, poorly paid, and have difficult working conditions. On top of this, they sometimes face pressure from the rich and powerful when solving a problem.

In the office and among the Indian community in Tokyo, word of our misfortune spread, and we quickly became known for the wrong reason. When I shared the information among colleagues in the office that "there was a burglary in my apartment," their first reaction was, "In India?". It was the usual stereotype that bad things only occurred in some countries. It annoyed me further. People found it very hard to believe that such things occurred in Tokyo, and since many of the employees in the headquarters were foreigners, they put themselves and their families on guard.

The reaction from our landlord and the police that the thieves were not Japanese was typical of their pride in themselves. It manifested twice – when police denied that any Japanese person was involved in the burglary and when the landlord falsely denied seeing the burglary in the CCTV footage. Had we accepted their word, we wouldn't have known the truth at all. In general, in society and in business, people attach high importance to *face-saving*. The need for pride, even in defeat, is what led to the unusual practice of *Harakiri* by the Warriors. Waiters at restaurants or hotel staff do not accept tips since they take pride in their work, and consider good quality service as their duty. Receiving tips would mean that they get paid extra for doing their work well. It took the honour away from their work, and hence they did not like being tipped.

Extremely Expensive Country

In the first few weeks in the country, as we settled down, it became clear how expensive it was. Here's some comparison to give you an idea

Cost in Indian Rupees (Re 80 = 1 US $ & Yen 150 = 1 US $)		
Item	**Japan**	**India**
An airport-city 70 km Taxi ride	10,000	1800
Bhindi/Okhra per kg.	500	50
A coconut	600	40
Watermelon	1000	75
Hair cut	1,800	250
Toll for a drive within the city	1,000	0

Even window shopping seemed like a loot!

So, why is it this way. Japan has a population of 127 million people. Roughly 70 percent of the land area is mountainous, which makes people live mostly around valleys, small plains, and along the coastal areas. Most people live in three large cities - Tokyo, Yokohama, and Osaka. These factors make land a scarce commodity and rentals extremely high. Where I lived, the apartment rent for 2400 square feet was $11,000 per month (in Shanghai, the same size apartment cost less than $4,000 in rent). Most people who worked in Tokyo city lived in the outskirts, commuting long hours to get to work. On average, the houses were small (600 square feet). Their focus on very high-quality (about which I discuss later in the book) adds to the cost structure. As an economy, Japan is partly socialist, resulting in organisations employing more people than, perhaps, required. Being highly prone to earthquakes, earthquake-proofing every structure becomes an added element of cost. All these add up and increase the cost.

Only a few companies, like IBM, could afford to locate their Asia-Pacific HQ in such an expensive city. It is also an indication of how huge IBM's business in Japan was. Later, the company could no longer afford it and shifted its Asia Pacific HQ to a cheaper location - Shanghai, resulting in me and my family moving from Tokyo to Shanghai.

Chapter 2

SOCIETY, CUSTOMS, TRADITION

Customs and traditions comprise a variety of things, from beliefs to art, dress, and people's behaviour. Every country develops its own unique way of life. Japanese culture is a set of values that places importance on social harmony and hard work. Up until the 10th century, Japanese culture was similar to Chinese culture, but the rise of the Samurai in the Heian period (794-1185) is known as the Golden age of Japanese history. This period saw the major import and further development of Chinese ideas in art, architecture, literature, and ritual, leading to a new and ultimately unique Japanese culture[3]. This, along with the Edo period (1603 to 1868), which practised isolation in trade and relations with other countries, when foreigners were banned from entering Japan, (and the Japanese were kept from leaving the country,) changed the rules of society. Even now, Japan has very tough immigration laws. Overall, the Japanese were influenced by the local Shintō religion, Buddhism, Confucianism, and the natural resources. While the Japanese lifestyle has been Westernised recently, Japanese people still do everything possible to preserve their rich cultural heritage[4]. Garden elements often represent spiritual beliefs, and there are detailed rules regarding their placement. Shintō, an ancient religion, honours invisible kami spirits in trees, rocks, and water[5].

What makes the Japanese different is not so much their customs and traditions but the fact that every single person – be it a child or a senior citizen – follows them without fail, every single time. For centuries, these have remained fairly unchanged without much adulteration from other influences.

In this chapter, I write about their:

- Population
- Religion
- Language
- Wedding
- Divorces

Population

As mentioned, their population is 127 million. A major demographic problem is that Japan has one of the lowest birth rates and among the highest life expectancy. Recession has been a significant issue the country has been facing for over 10 years. The number of employable people keeps reducing, and the number of people who live off savings or need support is increasing. One estimate[7] suggests that Japan's population could fall by 20% to levels below 100 million. So, population growth and mix are serious concerns in the country. Low rates of childbirth result in much lower business in childcare products, education, and housing etc. High life expectancy leads to a higher proportion of senior citizens who always spend/consume much less than youngsters. These factors have made economic growth a big challenge. To encourage childbirth, the government gave an incentive of 420,000 Yen (~US$3,000) per child for multiple childbirths.

Religion

If we break down a country's population by religion and express it in percentages, the resulting number will, naturally, add up to 100%. But, perhaps, not in Japan. It will be an arithmetically fallacious number of > 100%. That's because the Japanese practice multiple religions. According to the Government of Japan, as of 2018, 69.0% of the population practices Shintō, 66.7% practise Buddhism, 1.5% practise Christianity, and 6.2% practise other religions. This reflects a belief that Shintōism and Buddhism are sets of practices or a way of life that can be practised in conjunction with other beliefs. Religion to them has a social and ethical function and is not based on any specific ideology or doctrine. People generally do not hold or express intense religious feelings or religious identity (unlike in other parts of the world)[8]. Many people may say that they do not belong to any religion, yet it does not mean an indifference to religion. It is just that they do not identify themselves as belonging to a particular religion.

Shintō (literally meaning 'the way of *kami*') is the term used to refer to various religious myths, beliefs, and rituals that are indigenous to Japan. The foundation of Shintō is a belief in the existence of guardians or protecting deities, known as *kami*. It is thought that there are hundreds of kami that interrelate in multiple ways. Some kami have names and life narratives (like the sun goddess *Amaterasu*), some are seen as personifications of nature, and some are considered to be the spirits that animate natural features like waterfalls, large trees, or mountains. Each kami has varying degrees of power and is capable of gracious or destructive actions. Alongside *kami*, there are other kinds of spirits, such as messengers of individual *kami*. These messengers usually manifest in an animal form. For instance, the messenger of the great *kaminari* is depicted as a fox. Shrines for kami are often filled with statues of their messengers. Other spirits include those that perform ill-intended acts, as well as vengeful spirits who require pacification, often through Buddhist rituals or other means[9]. Trees, mountains, rivers all could be considered kami, and rituals are aimed at maintaining a balance between nature, humans, and kami. Buddhism arrived in Japan in the sixth century CE. Most Japanese families have a Buddhist altar of some sort in their homes.

"Goma": The Unmistakable Hindu Influence

My wife visited innumerable Buddhist Temples and Shintō Shrines. She would meticulously observe (and sometimes carefully imagine :) the resemblance of the rituals, idols, or temple structures to Hinduism. At Buddhist temples, the monks showed respect for us since we were Indo (Indians) and from the land of Buddha. Some of them, especially ones that had visited India, engaged in conversation with us, asking questions about India.

Two temple visits by the family stand out in memory. One was to the Narita-san temple, a Buddhist temple near Tokyo's airport Narita (in fact, the airport is named after the temple located in that suburb). As we entered it, we noticed priests performing a ritual called *Goma*, i.e., the Japanese word for the Hindu word *Homa*. And true to the name, it was amazingly similar to the Homa. Hindu influence had indeed travelled far and stayed. The priests sat around a "homa kundala" and were performing a fire ritual, putting wooden sticks (*Samith*) into the fire with chants that sounded, at least to our ears, Vedic. The fire symbolises the wisdom of the Buddha, and the wood sticks symbolise what is to be cleansed and released. The ceremony is performed with the purpose of destroying negative energies and detrimental thoughts and desires[10]. In true Japanese style, the wooden sticks were not twigs from trees, as in India, but rectangular sticks neatly manufactured in a factory. Prayers and wishes were written on these sticks.

Another temple visit was to Kyoto's famous Sanjusangendo, well-known for its 1001 statues of Kannon, the goddess of mercy. The temple was founded in 1164 and rebuilt a century later after the original structure had been destroyed in a fire. The name Sanjusangendo (literally "33 intervals") is derived from the number of intervals between the building's support columns, a traditional method of measuring the size of a building. In the centre of the main hall sits a large, wooden statue of a 1000-armed Kannon (Senju Kannon), with 11 heads to better witness the suffering of humans and with 1000 arms to better help them fight the suffering[11]. In addition to the thousand-armed Kannon statues, the hall displays 28 guardian deities whose origins lie in Hinduism and Sanskrit[12].

The deities at Sanjūsangen-dō trace their origins to Indian Dharmic mythology covering Hindu, Jain, and Buddhist Gods, and correspond to Varuna, Vishnu, Lakshmi, Brahma, Shiva, Garuda, Vayu, Narayana, Indra, and others[13].

Language

While the spoken language is Japanese, there are three different writing systems – Hiragana, Katakana, and Kanji. The Japanese script is based on 46 sounds. Hiragana and Katakana are two different ways to write the same set of sounds. They're the closest the Japanese language has to an alphabet. Characters generally represent a whole sound (like 'ki' or 'ra'), rather than individual letters (like 'k' or 'r'). Usually, Japanese words are written using Hiragana, while Katakana is used for words borrowed from other languages. So, for example, arigatou, Japanese for "thank you," is typically written あ り が と う (a ri ga to u) using Hiragana characters, whereas "America" is written ア メ リ カ (a me ri ka) using Katakana. Hiragana is the backbone of all Japanese learning. Unlike Hiragana and Katakana, the third writing style, Kanji, comprises Chinese characters. A single Kanji can be one word and not necessarily characters put together to make sounds and words. They are symbols that mean a whole word or idea[14].

Wedding

Apart from wedding practices, their system of giving gifts and the social malaise of parasite *singles* make this topic interesting.

Legally, both boys and girls can get married after 18. On average, as of 2020, the actual average age of marriage is 32 for men and 30 for women. Modern and western-style wedding ceremonies have crept into fashion and have influenced Japanese weddings. Ceremonies are held in Christian churches. Japanese traditions are less focused on. Despite being primarily a Buddhist nation, these Christian-style weddings are more of a style statement than a religious one. The bride and groom and their families exchange cups of sacred *sake* – a Shintō culture. Drinking from the same cup signifies the couple being united. Apart from song and dance, there is plenty to drink. Men don't wear two-piece suits as two indicates separation or division.

Monetary Gifts

It is common to give cash as a wedding gift to the couple. There are norms on how it is given. It has to be wrapped using a particular envelope made of a special type of cloth (called fukusa). The amounts involved can be large. Normally, the gift amount would be ¥30,000 (about $200) if you are a friend of the couple, ¥50,000 (about $350) if you are their boss or teacher, and ¥50,000 to ¥100,000 (about $350-$650) if you are a close relative. The cash gift needs to be crisp new currency notes. Used currency notes are given only at a funeral and so, are not to be used at the time of a wedding. The gift amount should not be divisible by two as it can signify a split among people and is hence considered inauspicious[15].

Wedding gift practices across the world can be strange. A friend of mine who lived in the Netherlands said that he and his teammates gifted a cow for their Dutch colleague's wedding. The American practice of creating a wedding registry that identifies the specific gift items that the couple would prefer is a good, practical one. But it can throw up some strange options. One of the gift items listed in the registry of a friend of ours was funny. The couple were to go to South Africa for their honeymoon and planned to hire a car there to commute between two cities. The car would require petrol/gasoline. So the couple listed 20 litres of petrol/gasoline as one of the gift items. By the time I accessed the registry, there were very few items left to pick, and I actually ended up gifting petrol. Imagine taking a cow or a can of petrol to a wedding hall and handing it over to the couple.

Women Remarriage

A woman is allowed to re-marry 100 days after divorce (earlier it was 6 months). This waiting time has been prescribed in the law to avoid doubts regarding the identity of the legally presumed father of a child conceived in that time period.

Japan's Marriage Crisis – "Parasite Singles"

Japan faces a social crisis by way of a large population of its men and women opting to remain unmarried. They live with their parents until marriage and face less immediate pressure to find a partner and are referred to as parasite singles. As of some years back, the percentage of unmarried men in that age group 30-34 was 47% and women 34%. Using a different age bracket, roughly a quarter of Japanese people between 20 and 49 are now single. And while people of this age routinely express a wish to get married, experts say that outdated social attitudes and increasing economic pressure are making tying the knot more and more difficult. The rate of cohabitation (sex) among unmarried adults was also low (2.3%), and only 2.3% of unmarried women had children[16]. In many other societies, the rate of unmarried may be higher, but so would the rate of cohabitation.

The cost-of-living, especially housing, is very prohibitive, and until marriage, single boys and girls remain with their parents. They depend on their parents, both physically and financially, for housing as well as daily necessities, such as laundry, cooking, and groceries. Despite having some form of income, the parasite singles tend to consider their entire earnings to be disposable. This form of economic parasitism leaves countless Japanese young adults with bountiful amounts of money to spend, which may explain how today, this community of people accounts for nearly 40 per cent of the luxury goods sales in Japan[17].

The reasons cited for remaining unmarried are many. The changing attitudes of women who want to be more independent but may be unable to find many men with such attitudes and women looking for more qualified husbands with better income levels than themselves are two such reasons. Those who cannot find them prefer to remain unmarried. Men's attitudes need to change faster. The number of people with non-permanent, i.e., contract jobs, has nearly tripled in the past 25 years, causing a level of uncertainty that society is not used to. After all, for a very long time, since companies did not practice laying off employees, people could work in an organisation forever without fear of job loss. Now, lower levels of income and an increase in the number of unstable jobs—with the fear of getting terminated at any time—weigh on people's minds and interfere with people's plans about getting married and having a family.

Divorces

As it turns out, unfortunately, my write-up on this topic will be much longer than on marriage. According to the Ministry of Health, Labour and Welfare, 35% of marriages in Japan end up in divorce. The rate is even higher among marriages between a Japanese and a non-Japanese—more than 50% fail, speaking volumes on how difficult it can be to maintain a cross-cultural relationship. Men's unchanging expectations that require women to take the lead on family affairs conflict with women pushing for shared responsibilities. Stagnant economic growth has made marriage and child-rearing a financial challenge for many couples[18].

As I searched for data on Japan's divorce rates, data on other countries appeared, and some of it was simply unbelievable. Divorce rates in South Korea is 46%, France 51%, Cuba 55%, Ukraine 70%. The countries with the lowest divorce rates were India 1%, Vietnam 7%, and Iran 14%[19]. These separation data around the world do not, include live-in relationships, which too break.

Interestingly, India has the lowest divorce rate—around 1%. Many will discount the goodness of this by citing the absence of a voice for women and the unequal nature of the husband-wife relationship. This is no doubt true. Given a choice, many women would have walked out of the marriage. But things are changing in urban and semi-urban India now, and hence the divorce rates too are increasing. So far, so good. But there must be some goodness too in the low rate in India. A social culture that prioritises the interest of the group (be it a joint family or even a nuclear family now) over individualism, strong family bonding, and a society that looked down upon divorcees meant that men and women learned to adjust to each other, avoiding a divorce. These must be reasons for the low rate. It can also, perhaps, be ascribed to children growing up with greater emotional support, available from both parents (as opposed to a single parent) and hence in a more stable home environment. But it's a topic not without debate, especially with the younger generation.

Silver Divorces - Divorces Among Senior Citizens

Silver divorces are those where couples divorce at an older age after being married for at least 20 years. Initially, such divorces in Japan were husband-instigated. But now, apparently, initiation by women too is on the increase. The "salaryman" has been the driving force behind Japan's post-war economic miracle, but unquestioning devotion to work made him a virtual stranger in his own home. Having given their best years and most of their time to their employers, many men enter retirement unable to relate well to their wives who have long since given up on their husbands. As men cut adrift from the routine of office life, they have no idea how to spend their newly acquired free time.

While the husband was working, it was just about acceptable because his wife has a proper role as a mother and housewife, but when he retires that all changes. Wives don't think they are being properly looked after, that their husbands simply regard them as the mother of their children. They quickly realise that they have been living separate lives for all those years[20]. Similarly, after barely spending time during younger years, suddenly the wives have to spend the entire day together with the husband – a transition they find difficult, leading to divorce. Around 2007, one bank introduced Divorce Loans to cover the costs of alimony, distribution of property, and, significantly, court action. The service, which was introduced after requests from customers, is expected to appeal to older couples, and women in particular, who can't afford the high interest charged by consumer loan firms[21].

Divorcing In-laws

Increasing numbers of Japanese widows are taking advantage of the procedure that allows them to sever ties with their in-laws in the form of the posthumous divorce. This reflects the fading of traditional views of the family as an institution where women join the family for life when they marry and shows a reluctance to bear the burden of caring for the deceased husband's ageing parents.

The process is simple. If a widow wants to break the remaining legal ties to her in-laws, all she needs to do is fill out an official form with just a few particulars, such as her name and address and the name of her deceased husband, and file it with the responsible office of the local municipal government together with personal identification and a copy of the family register recording her husband's death. The in-laws have no prior say in the matter, nor do they receive official notification of the break after the fact. And a widow (or widower) can file this termination report any time after a spouse's death; there is no waiting period or deadline for its submission[22].

Chapter 3

ONLY IN JAPAN

Most countries and cultures have something unique about them, more so, Japan. In the following pages, I write about some very diverse, unconnected topics such as:

- The shape of a watermelon
- Sumo wrestling
- Funeral gifts
- The traditional, famous tea ceremony
- Tsunami and their amazing response
- Courteous cab drivers
- Hiroshima
- Royalty and
- Harakiri

The Shape of A Watermelon

Watermelons, being round in shape, occupy a lot of storage space in refrigerators and during transport. So here's their solution to the problem – modify its shape, make it cube-shaped (see picture). This way, storage and transport become much more space and cost-efficient. The fruit is not genetically modified to this shape. Instead, they put a cube-shaped 'case' around the baby melon to ensure that it grows and finishes as a cube.

Sumo Wrestling

Our family watched a Sumo wrestling tournament in Ryogoku, Tokyo. It was a day-long event of at least 60-70 matches, each of which, on average, somewhat annoyingly, lasted just 8-10 seconds. The longest one was about 40 seconds. When the two wrestlers come onto the ring, the build-up to each fight comprises slapping their chest and thighs in a show of strength and throwing salt (see picture). This took more than a minute but the fight itself was just a few seconds, with the winner pushing the losing contestant out of the ring. On average, a wrestler weighs 150-200 kgs (the 3 heaviest sumo wrestlers weighed between 277 kg to 292 kg).[23] It was quite a sight, seeing 200-kilo huge, mountainous men fight, wearing close to nothing. As in several other sports, there were allegations of drug usage and match-fixing.

Sumo wrestling is one of the oldest sports, originating about 1,500 years, and was entwined with Shintō religious ritual when it was performed at shrines to ensure a bountiful harvest and to honour the spirits – known as kami, the Shintō religious belief about which we read earlier. The canopy that hangs over the wrestling ring is modelled after the roof of a Shintō shrine, indicating that the ring itself is a holy place.

The sumo wrestler's life is possibly the most regimented and disciplined of any athlete in the world, and life in a sumo stable is incredibly hard. The sumobeya, or stable, is where the wrestlers live, eat, train, and sleep throughout their career. Married wrestlers are allowed to live independently. An average stable houses 15 wrestlers and is arranged according to a strict hierarchy. Life is hardest for junior wrestlers who are expected to get up early and cook, clean, serve food, and generally wait on the higher-ranked wrestlers. In practices that resemble Army life, they endure high physical activity, done to toughen them up. This is part and parcel of sumo culture and something that young wrestlers know to expect.

In addition to the strict routine governing their training schedule, sumo wrestlers are expected to control their demeanour and personality in public. Rules delineate that when out and about, wrestlers must be self-effacing and softly spoken, and during tournaments, they should refrain from showing joy at winning or disappointment at losing. No amateur dramatics or self-congratulatory gloating here[24].

What gives them their body size? Wrestling and boxing have divisions by weight, but Sumo has no weight-based classification. So sumo wrestlers want to be as big as possible so they can use their weight to push their opponent out of the ring. Their diet includes a special food called chankonabe - a stew served in a giant pot (nabe), a type of Japanese nabe (hot pot), which I think is similar to a stew (but with more broth). It is traditionally eaten by sumo wrestlers, is high in protein, and is usually served in massive quantities as part of a weight-gain diet for sumo wrestlers. They eat this meal pretty regularly with different ingredients. The characteristic of this hot pot is that there is no specific "recipe". And unlike other varieties of Japanese hot pot meals, meats, seafood, vegetables, and pretty much everything can be thrown into the hot pot[25].

Funeral Gifts

The Japanese have a distinctive custom of gifting money to the bereaved family during a funeral. The quantum of the gift depends on how close the family is and one's own social status. An expatriate colleague of mine, who attended one, mentioned that a parent of a person in his own team passed away and upon inquiry, he was told that since it was somebody really close to him in the office, $250 would be a reasonable amount. He, gave the sum as a gift. The legacy of this practice is a few hundred years old when the gift was intended to provide financial help to the family for the months/year following the funeral. The cash has to be in the form of used notes, not crisp new ones, because new notes signify that you were perhaps expecting the event and prepared for it. These notes must be presented in an appropriate envelope. There are norms relating to how the inner and outer parts of the envelope should be and how words should be written[26].

At the funeral, there is strict etiquette on how to talk to family, when to talk, and so on. After cremation, they remove the bones with a special pair of long chopsticks. A professional assists the family at the beginning of the kotsuage process, giving them an introduction to the bones in different sections of the remains. Then, the family is left to complete this process. It is also common for the bone fragments to be passed from chopsticks to chopsticks, i.e., person to person, among family members. The family picks through the fragments starting at the feet and moving upwards. The ashes and bones are placed into the urn starting with the feet so that the body is feet-down in the urn, like a natural human stance when the person is alive. Once this process is complete, the urn stays within the family's shrine for anywhere from 30 to 50 days depending on the region of Japan (this is different from the Indian system, where the ashes are never brought home). It is considered important for these ashes to rest up to 50 days at the family's shrine before they're brought to the cemetery. From there, it's taken to a graveyard for the ashes to be buried. Because some families have multiple shrines, multiple urns are common. The ashes are distributed evenly amongst them, and they'll go to different shrines within the family[27].

Over 90% of death rituals performed are Buddhist. The funeral is performed by a Buddhist priest, allowing attendants to remember, mourn, and seek closure for the deceased as they transition from life to the afterlife.

Tea Ceremony

The four of us went for a Japanese Tea Ceremony, a highly spoken about tradition in the country. This event is unique because of a distinctive technique involved in the use of equipment, the process of preparation, and drinking. There is a separate room for each individual or family, unlike a traditional restaurant. The menu was elaborate: a very small marble-sized sweet item and a very small cup of tea. It took all of 45 minutes to complete the ceremony. There was a lot of fuss about the procedure, as we were taught how to hold the cup, how to turn it, twist it, sip it making noise, blah, blah. It cost 3,000 Yen per cup ($ 20). There are places where this ceremony could cost 15,000 Yen ($ 100) per person.

The Japanese Tea Ceremony evolved under the influence of Zen Buddhism and aims to attain a perfect balance between nature and the human soul. This ceremony is conducted by a trained master and is done by performing the task of making tea in a series of graceful movements, making it beautiful to watch[28]. The tea ceremony was introduced to Japan by a Buddhist monk named Eisai, who also introduced Zen Buddhism to Japan. Over time, Zen monks incorporated tea into Zen practice, paying attention to every detail of its creation and consumption. There are a lot of similarities between the main principles of the tea ceremony (harmony, respect, tranquillity) and the philosophy of Zen (mindfulness, transience, acceptance). Tea ceremony masters are not just trained in a specific type of tea making, but more importantly in Zen philosophy[29]. It is preferable to read about the ceremony before going there, which is something we did not do, making us wonder what the hype was all about and why preparing and consuming a cup of tea required so much time. It was only later that we learned about its significance. The entire preparation and drinking process is a form of meditation. Therefore, the positive values are applied to the entire ceremony without only focusing on the tea as the end product.

Tsunami and Extreme Discpline

On March 11, 2011, Japan experienced the strongest earthquake in its recorded history. The earthquake struck below the North Pacific, 130 kilometres (81 miles) East of Sendai, the largest city in the Tohoku region, a northern part of the island of Honshu. A tsunami is a series of powerful waves caused by the displacement of a large body of water. Most tsunamis, like this one that formed off Tohoku, are triggered by underwater tectonic activity, such as earthquakes and volcanic eruptions. The Tohoku Tsunami produced waves of up to 40 metres (132 feet) high; more than 450,000 people became homeless as a result of the tsunami, and more than 15,500 people died. The tsunami also severely crippled the infrastructure. In addition to the thousands of destroyed homes, businesses, roads, and railways, the tsunami caused the meltdown of three nuclear reactors at the Fukushima Daiichi Nuclear Power Plant and forced thousands of people to evacuate their homes and businesses[30].

But natural disasters occur everywhere. When it does, in Japan, it is the way in which they respond that is quite extraordinary. We all know the typical response immediately after a tragedy – chaos, looting, violence, mob mentality, and other look-out-for-yourself behaviour. But in Japan, there were no signs of looting or violence. A picture attached[31] tells the story. People can be seen waiting in a very orderly way to collect relief material for themselves and their family. There was no water, gas, or electricity, and yet people remained calm and disciplined, without any panic. Looting simply does not take place in Japan. Japanese have a sense of being first and foremost responsible to the community (source: http://googl/oacpa). The normal course of action is to enforce order and crowd control, but since there is no mob-like behavior, it does not distract or take away key government personnel from truly pressing needs, allowing medical and security personnel to focus on the real victims of the disaster[32]. Such discipline is also a symbol of the people's faith in the ability of the government to take care of them.

Courteous Cabbies

Cabs in Japan are extremely clean and almost always look new on the exterior. I cannot remember a cab with dirty interiors or faded seat covers. The doors are centrally operated by the driver and can be opened and closed only by him, using buttons. Cab drivers follow one very polite and customer-friendly practice. When a passenger takes a taxi and shows the driver the address, the driver considers it his responsibility to reach that place by the shortest route possible. So, if upon reaching that locality, he is not able to go directly to the desired destination and has to go around searching, he will stop the taxi meter when the search starts (those were non-GPS days). He considers the additional time and commute to be his fault and something that a customer cannot be charged for. It's such a nice practice, especially in the cab driver community, many of whom, perhaps due to the stressful nature of their job, can be quite rude – be it Delhi, Rio, or New York. By the way, taxi drivers in Japan never refuse a customer. It is considered to be very impolite.

Hiroshima

In instalments, all four members of my family went to Hiroshima to see the city that was brutally bombed. The museum there is both sobering and dignified. The entire presentation at the museum complex is extremely well done with detailed explanations of how a nuclear bomb dissipates energy, the impact on its population of the bomb at the time it is dropped and 5 or 10 years later, and the city's subsequent slow recovery. The museum and park carry no signs or language of rancour or bitterness against the perpetrators.

We were numbed by exhibits in the museum that displayed pictures of the bombing and its aftermath, highlighting the scale of destruction (60,000 buildings were destroyed in one go) and showing how countless people were scarred for life by radiation. The nuclear bomb (named "Little Boy") killed 150,000 people, half of whom died on the spot while the balance died over the next one year, suffering from the effects of burns and radiation. Many were killed due to birth defects and cancer that occurred for many years after the bombing. Such a disastrous impact on humans? One wonders why there was a second, even more lethal plutonium bomb, named "Fat Man", dropped in Nagasaki? Another 150,000-200,000 people were killed in this attack. The aircraft that dropped these bombs are displayed in a museum in Washington. Such a display could be a symbol of power and retaliation, or intended to be a sobering reminder of a not-so-proud moment in history.

Royalty

Post-World War II, royalty has remained more of a European custom than an Asian one – with one exception: Japan. The Emperor of Japan is the Head of State. Emperor Showa was the 124th Emperor of Japan and performed this role for one of the longest periods, from 1926 to 1989. His son, Akihito, took over from him in 1989. In 2018, he abdicated the throne, citing old age - the first such act in over 200 years, paving the way for his son, Prince Naruhito. The role of the Emperor is largely ceremonial, yet Emperor Akihito is not just respected but revered (similar to how the erstwhile princely community in India is still looked up to by villagers). December 23rd is Emperor Akihito's birthday and is a big day. Thousands of people visit the palace and form long queues to greet him. December 23rd is a holiday in Japan. December 25th is not.

Harakiri

I now switch gears and take you 500 years back in time.

A ritual for suicide? Harakiri (*Hara* meaning stomach, *kiri* is cutting) has its roots in 12th-century Japanese samurai warrior culture. Rather than be captured, a defeated swordsman would kill himself in a certain way- by stabbing the left belly, drawing the blade to the right and then pulling upwards. Practised by defeated samurai warriors, it was meant as atonement and a way of winning back some measure of honour even in defeat. There were other reasons for committing Harakiri, such as to atone for botching an assignment, out of grief over a leader's death, or as a form of protest for a larger cause. Some Emperors sent a messenger to give a ceremonial dagger to the person they wanted dead. The unlucky recipient had no choice but to kill himself, but because the death was self-inflicted through Harakiri, it was considered more honourable than an execution by the Emperor or government. The practice of Harakiri was abolished in 1868.

I conclude this chapter with some assorted material.

Hachiko: The Iconic Dog

The Shibuya is a suburb in Tokyo, and the Shibuya railway station is an important part of the city's train network. The road crossing just outside the station is one of the busiest road crossings in the country, with thousands of people using it every minute. A statue of a dog named Hachiko is also very famous. In the late 1920s and 1930s, every day, Hachiko would come to the station to meet its master, Ueno, when he returned from work, and would walk back home with him. But Ueno died. In an amazing display of affection and loyalty, even after his death, Hachiko would come to the station at the same time, every single day, to receive him, wait for him to come, and after some time, return home. In honour of such immense love and affection, a statue of the dog was built at the station.

The Japanese, especially women, love pets. Small, almost cat-sized, dogs were their favourite breed. According to a 2020 customer survey of a pet insurance company, pet owners in Japan spend an average of about 300,000 Yen ($2,000) annually on a dog and 160,000 Yen ($1,100) on a cat[33], including on boutiques and health centres. The dogs never barked or ran around – Japanese discipline at its best.

A "Mobile" Building

Ever heard of a building being moved? There was a railway station in interior Japan where the total area of the station was large, but it had just a small structure in the middle of it, resulting in a lot of unused space. The structure was considered heritage. They wanted to make better use of the space but were sensitive to the heritage building not being demolished. So, as a solution for creating more construction space, they simply moved the building to one side of the land area. It was unheard of and truly amazing.

Babyishness

In advertisements, women use a baby-like voice. Even visuals would be of making baby-like gestures. The female voice in train announcements would sound as if a 6-year-old was speaking. Sometimes women's clothing looked that way too.

Chapter 4

CULTURE

In this chapter, I share their culture and explore how this society is different from those in other countries. I write about aspects that truly define the Japanese. People would certainly have heard about many of these, and so, for the reader to get a better feel, I will lace it with several personal anecdotes. The topics that I will cover are:

- Politeness and Respect
- An obsession with quality
- Precision
- Punctuality and
- Discipline

Politeness and Respect

Our family was returning to Tokyo from a holiday. A friend of ours had asked us to hand a gift packet to his friend a Japanese gentleman in Tokyo, who would meet us at the airport to collect it. When we landed, he was there in the airport arrival area, waiting with a name card. We greeted each other and engaged in some courtesy talk for a few minutes.

I introduced my family, and he, in turn, spoke briefly about himself before we handed over the packet. It was time for both of us to go our respective ways, but he kept standing there. There was some silence between us because, after all, how much can you talk to a complete stranger. Gauging the uneasiness, he **explained** the reason why he was still waiting to leave. What we had not noticed when we were conversing with him was that my younger son had gone away to the rest-room. The Japanese gentleman said that he was waiting for my son to return because it would be bad manners and impolite to walk away without saying **goodbye** and taking leave of each one of us, including my 9-year-old son. Wow. I don't even think such a thought would have occurred to people from any other country.

People are very polite - in words and in many routine actions. A nation of over 100 million people, it appeared, never lost their temper. Everyone was always calm and controlled. A friend of mine described the society as having "mastery over emotions." When learning the Japanese language, the polite way of saying, asking, and commenting is specifically taught. At a shop, their staff would say Arigato Gozaimasu (thank you) at every stage of the purchase process – trial, selection, billing, payment, and collection. Service to customers at the shop would be uniformly courteous - independent of how much they bought. In many countries, perhaps most for that matter, the behaviour of the staff would be based on their judgement of how much the customer is likely to buy, but not in this country. As a tourist, when we required directions to a place and asked a shopkeeper, he/she would not just give directions - they would leave their shop and walk with us as far as they could, taking us as close to our destination as possible, without our having to guess the directions any further or ask someone else.

While walking on the footpath, if the path is narrow and people in front of you block the pathway, unless you are in a hurry, it would be considered poor manners to ask them to make way for you and overtake them. Unlike other countries, you don't say "excuse me" to walk past them, but instead simply wait until the people in front observe you and give way. Btw, the Japanese word for "excuse me" is sumimasen. I thought it sounded so much like the name of the Indian actress Sushmita Sen!

Here are few more observations that showcase their politeness:

At a traffic signal, if the light turns green for vehicles, and if at that time a pedestrian is still crossing the road, to avoid any stress to the pedestrian, drivers in all lanes in that direction, including the lanes that the person has already crossed, will wait for him/her to finish crossing the road, and only then start moving.

To get a haircut done, one has to make an appointment with the barber shop. On one occasion, when I arrived at the shop at the appointed time, I was told that due to some confusion, my slot was double-booked, and a haircut was not possible. I was asked to come after a few hours. Feeling sorry for this mistake, every single one of the 5-6 staff there stopped their work for a few seconds, bowed, and apologised to me in unison. After a few hours, when I went there at the revised time, as soon as I entered the shop, each staff member again bowed, apologised, and welcomed me.

The Suffix "San" and Bowing

Two very important practices of social etiquette and respect are bowing and adding the suffix 'san' to a name – like ji in India. No one ever forgets to add san to a name, even while referring to children. In India too, we use suffixes like ji in Hindi, garu in Telugu, and bhai/baen in Gujarati, to address people respectfully, but with the exception perhaps of Gujaratis who almost always use it, we don't use it unfailingly. In Japan, it is used 100% of the time. If an institution or an element of nature deserves respect, san is used for it too. Their favourite mountain, Mt Fuji, is referred to as Fuji-san and the Narita temple as Narita-san.

Talking of names and san, at the office, my name Ravi used to be pronounced as "Laabi" and I will be called as "Laabi-san" since they use L for R, R for L, and B for V! This mix-up in pronunciation can be humorous. Once in an aircraft that we were flying, the hostess announced that the aircraft "will land in the right lane". I was puzzled – why would it matter to me if it landed on the left or the right lane? I kept looking outside the window, noticed that it was drizzling and then realised that when she said right lane, she meant that the aircraft would land in light rain!

To them, the practice of bowing to people is a bit like breathing. Bowing is their method of greeting, not a handshake. It's an expression of respect, gratitude and appreciation. When they walk past a person they knew, they would bow, even if only mildly. On average, a Japanese person, businessman or employee bows 100 times a day. Depending on the status of the person one is greeting, the extent of bowing or bending, would be 15 – 90 degrees. If a very senior person was leaving the room or say a venue, the others would bow 90 degrees and remain bowed till that person's car started moving away.

An Obsession with Quality

In our apartment, there was a very small water seepage in one of the walls. The plumbing company made three visits before repairing it. First, a team of two people came home.

One of them spent time understanding the problem and made notes, and another took pictures of the wall. The next day, another team of two came and stood in the street staring at the exterior wall of the building. Perplexed about strangers staring at our apartment, we inquired with our landlord as to what was happening. He informed us that it was a team of civil engineers checking from the outside for possible reasons for the seepage. Thus, multiple visits were made to study the seepage from different angles with the aim of not just repairing it but getting to the root cause and ensuring that it never occurred again. Only on the 3rd visit did they actually repair it. In any other country, the repair would take one quick visit to fix the problem. For the repair itself, the plumber made elaborate preparations before repairing it (see picture). Before starting the work, he put plastic sheets in every area that debris could potentially fall during the repair. It would appear that they overdo things, but the seriousness attached even to a small defect was admirable to watch, reflecting a truly zero-tolerance culture.

Incidentally, the seepage itself was very small. The reason we complained to the landlord was that we were cautioned by people that while vacating the house, the landlord would go around the house, literally carrying a magnifying glass, checking for any damages and would levy a penalty on the tenant. So we did not want this to become a big issue later. This was no empty threat. It happened with one of my colleagues in the office. She lived in an apartment with her two dogs. When she vacated, the landlord surveyed the house and noted that her dogs had scratched and caused damage to the carpets and walls. He levied a penalty of US$22,000 (yes!) for the damages. The lady was in tears as she could simply not afford that kind of money. But, the landlord refused to negotiate and held back the deposit paid by the company. She approached the company for monetary help, and the company agreed to bear 50% of the penalty.

When people say, "Made in Japan", the first thought that occurs to everyone world-over is "exceptional quality". Several behavioural traits of their society cause this - a maniacal focus on quality, an ability to think through and plan every detail, building efficiency into everything and seeking extreme precision.

Quality is an obsession, not just a desire. Nothing we saw in two years was less than high-quality. Be it goods, services, roads, footpaths, the transport system, et al, it would be of high-quality by thinking through every aspect of design, efficiency, durability, customer convenience, and space-saving. The building that we lived in was over 20 years old, yet the fittings and electrical items functioned perfectly. This quality focus is what has made global giants of Sony, Toyota, Mitsubishi, Honda, Canon, Nikon, Hitachi, Noritake, and many more. We've all enjoyed their products. The consumers there are very demanding in not just product quality but also service, during and after sale. At shops, it is common to have more salespersons than what's required to ensure that every customer need is promptly attended to.

A cultural comparison of the quality-cost equation between India and Japan is interesting. Japan prioritises quality above all, and cost is the second priority. In India, historically, due to much lower income levels and affordability issues, low cost is the first priority, even if quality has to be compromised (although, with growing income levels, this is changing now).

An Eye for Detail and Thinking Through Everything

Let me start with a few examples of this:

We were once buying chestnuts from a street-side vendor. Nuts usually have a hard shell, sometimes requiring the need for sharp nails or using one's teeth to open them. When handing over the chestnuts, the vendor gave a small plastic shell-opener. It was shaped just like our thumb with a small dent to place the thumb in and with sharp edges to break open the shell easily.

World-over, when writing a postal address, people begin with the name of the receiver and end with the postal code:

Mrs ATZ
101, Lovely apartment,
Lonely street
Crowded city
Postal code 415161
Country X

But as we know, postmen always read it in reverse order, i.e., first the receiver's country, then the city and postal code, and then which area, street, home, and receiver's name. We write top-down, but the postmen read it bottom-up. In Japan, addresses are written the way the postmen read it – i.e., start with the country name and end with the receiver's name. A simple difference in practice that makes it more practical.

While entering temples, as in India, as a mark of hygiene and respect, footwear has to be removed. In doing so, we usually leave it facing the temple, but when we complete the temple visit and return to the gate, we need to flip it around to wear it or we turn ourselves after wearing it. To avoid this, when devotees are inside the temple, some temples had volunteers who reversed the direction of the footwear to make it just that little extra easier for you to wear it and exit. It's no doubt a trivial thing, but this is the level of attention to detail that their culture pays in ensuring convenience.

When building a product or service, they study the different steps (actions) the customer would take in the process of buying a product, such as their buying behaviour when at the store, how they would carry something after its purchase, its various uses and its disposal. They then build these into the product feature and selling process.

Efficiency

They strive to build in efficiency into everything. I mentioned earlier about how efficient our house agent was when we were searching for an apartment. Here are a few more examples:

Can four cars be parked in the space of one? When walking on a footpath, I once noticed cars entering and leaving a building with a small entrance that looked neither like a garage nor a car park. It had a 60-foot high wall with only a few windows. Curious, I peeped in and noticed something amazing. The building with a floor space of maybe 3,000 square feet had a Ferris wheel (merry-go-round) to move cars up and down. Within this small floor area, where no more than a few cars could otherwise be parked, at least 20 cars were parked. This is how it worked. The car would first be placed on a flat iron sheet at the entrance. The Ferris wheel would then move the car up, making space for the next car, exactly the way a merry-go-round works at entertainment parks. When it was time to hand the car back to its owner, the wheel would revolve to bring the car from wherever it was and place it back at the entrance. But, there was one challenge. Once the car was at floor level, the driver would have to reverse the car from the building to enter the road, which can be cumbersome in the narrow roads of Tokyo. They had a smart solution for this. The car that had to exit would be placed on a **turntable** which then turned the car 180 degrees to face the road so that the driver could drive forward easily without going through the pain of reversing it and disturbing the flow of traffic on the road.

A haircut for small boys (age 2-5) is often a pain. They feel scared, cry and move around constantly, making the process time-consuming. It will also sometimes lead to minor cuts and bruises. For long, their solution to this was to put a small TV screen in front of the child and play a cartoon video. The boys, engrossed in the cartoon, let the barber cut freely, without any disturbance and finish the haircut easily and quickly.

While walking on a footpath, we once noticed two people staring at a small TV screen. We were wondering what they were doing in the middle of the footpath. It appears they were municipal staff trying to identify the source of leakage of a drainage pipe. Instead of digging a large portion of the pavement to find out where the problem was, they made one small hole and put an electronic wire with a camera into it. The wire was passed along the drainage, and the camera located the source of the problem - similar to an endoscopy done on our stomach to diagnose an illness. This ensured that they needed to dig only one particular spot without disturbing the rest of the area.

Precision

Precision is embedded into everything. The culture itself is to be precise. At a shop, if the bill was 1203 Yen, even if it is more convenient to round off to 1200 or 1205, we had to pay 1203. If it meant paying 1300 Yen and **receiving** 97 Yen in return, it had to be done. 1203 is, simply, 1203. To help customers who would not have small change – say 3 Yen, at all shops, at the billing counter, there would be a box with loose change, from which we could pick up coins free, and use it to pay the exact amount. Incidentally, the currency of Japan has only a single unit Yen i.e., there is no subdivision, like Rupee and Paise or dollar and cents, and so everything is expressed in the equivalent of paise or cents. 1203 Yen in India would be Rs 12.03.

Precision is achieved when you understand something as-is, without imagining something else. It's not possible if we make something subject to, if or when. It is this culture, and the commitment to quality, that makes a train of 6.22 pm always come in exactly at 6.22, time after time, day-in and day-out. Such predictability makes life so much easier.

Punctuality

Punctuality and precision are absolute hallmarks of their culture – there is no generalisation, 'range' or rounding-off. During our stay in Tokyo, as is common, we used public transport (trains, buses, and cabs), since owning a car was very expensive, parking fees and tolls prohibitive, and traffic very heavy. The Tokyo train network comprises 14 different train lines. The coordination was so superb that, during the many trips we made over our two years' stay, not one single train was late by even 1 minute. If a train had to arrive at 7.36 am or 8.47 pm, it would arrive precisely at that time. You would have heard the old joke/fact that in Japan, no employee can make an excuse of "delay in train service" for coming late to the office. Trains, buses, meetings in the office, nothing ever came or started late. For an 11 am meeting or social function, they will make it a point to arrive early and wait until it is 11 and then enter the meeting room or host's house. If an item has to be home-delivered, they would commit time precisely - like "8 days from now, at 10.15 am", and it would arrive exactly then.

How does India fare in comparison? Indians have a slightly different philosophy on punctuality:

"Why waste time being punctual?"

We believe in flexibility – not for the host, but for the guest. If there is a dinner scheduled at 7 pm, at home or outside, most guests will arrive somewhere between 7.45 pm and 8.30 pm. In Bengaluru (Bangalore), where I live, they will quickly blame its infamous traffic for their delayed arrival. For the same dinner, however, foreigners will arrive roughly around the scheduled time of 7 pm. Do they use hot-air-balloons to avoid traffic? Not really. And, no matter how much people curse Bangalore's traffic, it certainly does not indulge in racial discrimination. It simply ill-treats all motorists. Let's give the devil its due.

Discipline

The culture of following every rule in every rule book makes the country one of the most disciplined societies in the world. It is discipline that helps achieve high-quality, precision, punctuality, a great eye for detail, efficiency, and consistent respect.

I was trying to compare a few cultures on the aspect of discipline. In India, there is a lot of order and discipline within the family. We are expected to follow norms and tradition, we generally do that, and by and large, there is order. But once we leave the house and hit the street, it is a free-for-all. We cause and face all the ills of a society that is poor on discipline – well reflected in traffic, hygiene, queuing etc. In America, it seems the opposite – very disciplined in public and high on compliance, but at home and in the family, individualism and an I-do-what-I-think-right approach gets priority. Japan, on the other hand, has both high discipline at home and outside.

Boon or Bane?

Unfortunately, the very high levels of discipline, along with the Japanese way of doing everything, impose a level of rigidity in society. But extreme levels of discipline can have psychological implications and impose a burden. To be expected to do everything in exactly the same way, every single time, all the time makes life somewhat robotic. Behaviourally, they are expected to keep their emotions always under check. Even laughing loudly is not considered good manners. If Indians are argumentative and noisy and we sometimes don't like that, the Japanese are the opposite – extremely calm and silent. And as they say, silence can be deafening! But discipline being a strength and a weakness fits into my general belief about life, that our strengths are also our weaknesses. For example, many pushy and aggressive salespeople in the office are disliked for their nature, but their aggressive nature is also the reason for their success in making customers buy. Some people who are calm and polite are loved, but this calmness prevents them from taking actions or showing toughness when they need to. I suppose it's about achieving the right balance in everything.

The custom of having drinks with business associates or office colleagues after office hours many days a week throughout the year curtails rest and family time. And who wants trains to be so punctual. I mean, what's the fun if you can't go late to work and blame it on traffic or public transport!

1001 images of Kannon at the Sanjusangendo temple

Cube shaped watermelons

*The ritual of spraying salt by
a Sumo wrestler before the contest*

A disciplined crowd collecting food after the Tsunami

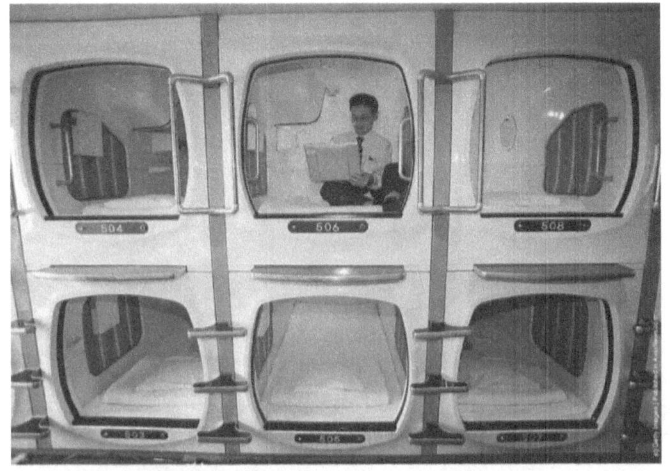

'Rooms' in a capsule hotel, used for overnight stay.

Left: A watch recovered from the ruins of Hiroshima, with the time frozen at the exact time (8.15 am) of the bombing on Aug 6, 1945. Right: My son and classmate with Matsubara-san, a survivor of the bombing.

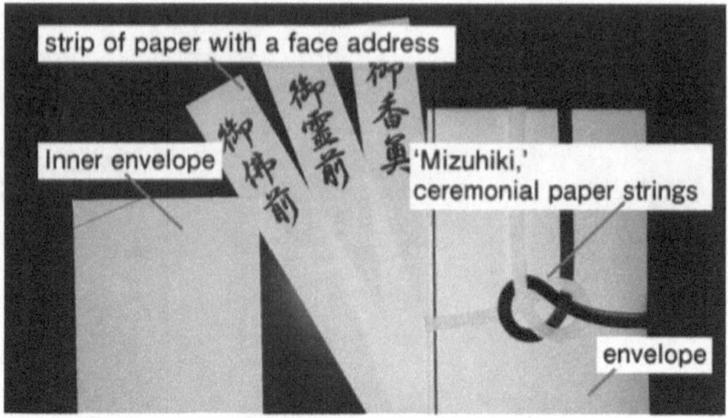

*The specific type of envelope in which
a funeral cash gift is usually packaged*

*At the rear right, you can see a cubicle made of
plastic sheets, to ensure that small particles of debris
would not fly around*

Chapter 5

BUSINESS CUSTOMS AND ETIQUETTE

This chapter outlines the behavioural aspects of people at work and in business, such as:

- Importance of business relationships and face-saving
- Work culture
- Group solidarity
- Meeting ettiquette
- Superstitions in business
- Politeness and efficiency at work
- Business and societal challenges, and
- What the Japanese think about Indians

Relationship-Based Business

Like in India and most Asian societies, relationships are extremely important in business. Building and sustaining business relationships requires meticulously cultivating business associates over time, necessitating regular wining, dining, or golfing. The business culture tends to focus on the relationships among associates instead of the benefits of a deal. Business deals are very rarely closed in the first meeting, so walking away empty-handed after a meeting is not something to be unduly worried about. Businesses tend to plan for the long term, preferring to get to know you, your products, and services before establishing a business deal – much like making friends or courting.

The need for trust in business is overriding. They go to great lengths to protect their word. The word or verbal agreements are more important than what's written in a contract, and so it is common for businesses to go beyond the contract if required to complete a project or meet customer requirements. It is a low-litigation society, and they prefer to settle disagreements through mutual discussion. In the office I worked in, many Westerners found it hard to understand how verbal discussions and commitments were given more importance than a written agreement. This response was not surprising, I suppose, because some Westerners believe most of their practices to be superior to those of others anyway. It's a bit of a "my way or the highway" approach.

Japanese people value modesty. During a business meeting, it is important to take this into consideration and speak in a calm tone without making too much commotion. Similarly, it is incorrect to put pressure on the host or the other party to make a decision on the spot.

They are known to avoid direct statements, so instead of saying no, they may use phrases like "it is difficult" or "we'll think about it". They may also change the topic or pretend not to understand. For someone unfamiliar with this nature, their responses can be misinterpreted as rude or indifferent. Although these phrases seem hopeful, they are also a polite and indirect way of saying "no"[34].

Face-saving and Johatsu

Face-saving is an important part of societal behaviour, in personal life and in business. Individuals worry about the loss of face and about what others think or speak of them, making them risk-averse and less willing to do things new or different, fearing that society, especially their group, will talk badly or label them. Face-saving is so important in the country that a few people who lose jobs or have failed in business 'evaporate'. Léna Mauger, a French journalist, had investigated the phenomenon of Johatsu, or evaporated people. As per her book, every year, nearly one hundred thousand people vanish without a trace. People become Johatsu for a number of reasons, including sexual impropriety, and a desire for isolation. Sometimes, it is used to escape domestic violence, gambling debt, religious cults, stalkers, employers, and difficult family situations. The shame of job loss, divorce, and even failing an exam can also motivate people to disappear. In some cases, becoming Johatsu is a way to just have a fresh start. When they disappear, they can abandon their former residences, jobs, families, names, and even appearances. This phenomenon apparently exists all over the world, such as the United States, China, South Korea, the United Kingdom, and Germany. However, it is likely more prevalent in Japan, given certain cultural factors. Detective agencies are sometimes used to find people who have become Johatsu...

Work Culture

For decades, especially post world war II, their work culture and philosophy was "employer-first and family second". They return home very late from work every day, leading to a social problem. We read earlier about the problem of post-retirement divorces. It was a practice for people to leave the office only after the boss leaves and also avoid leaving before their group/peers – all out of politeness. There are suicides driven by over-work (Karoshi). Laws have been introduced over the years to reduce work hours and reduce stress, but on the ground, the culture is taking time to change.

To cater to people who frequently stay very late in the office and prefer to avoid long commutes back home, there were Capsule hotels in Tokyo. The 'rooms' are in the form of very small capsule-sized areas fitted with a single bed and a small TV (see picture). Each cubicle has space to lie down and is of just about enough height to sit. To give you an idea, the total space per capsule would be similar to the lower berth of a 2-tier train in India. Since customers come into these hotels at the end of a long working day, their clothes would be dirty, and so the hotel would wash and dry them overnight and keep them ready before the customer left for the office the next morning.

Group Solidarity

It is widely known that Japan is a group-oriented culture where group solidarity is often valued over individualism. As their saying goes, "A single arrow is easily broken, but not ten in a bundle." This cultural mindset influences certain behaviours, such as how praise is received. While Western cultures may value individual contributions and strongly believe in recognition and individual praise, the opposite can be true in Japan. Singling out an individual in the group for special recognition, no matter how helpful he or she is to you, may likely embarrass that individual. When doing business, the team concept is crucial for Japanese employees, so when giving credit in public, it is directed to the entire group[35].

It is common for colleagues in their groups to go together for a meal, a night out in the town, or drinks after-office-hours (Thank God, I was not born Japanese, as my policy has always been that I do not drink after-office-hours!). When colleagues drink or dine together, the practice is to share the cost in proportion to their seniority—i.e., based on their ability to pay. Drinking with subordinates is common since they tend to share their views more openly than in the office.

However, in recent years, there has been a gradual shift towards individualism, especially among the younger generation. This change is influenced by factors such as increased globalisation. Now, young professionals are more inclined to prioritise personal aspirations, which can sometimes clash with traditional, group-oriented expectations.

The 2011 earthquake and the Covid pandemic have brought about notable changes in the work culture. To quote a Japanese national, "Now, there is increased focus on work-life balance and family connections. The significant impact of the disaster on communities and individuals seemed to have shocked many people nationwide, influencing their perceptions of life. As a result, individuals who had been leaning towards a capitalistic and results-driven work ethic have begun reconsidering their current job approaches. They started seeking workplace environments that allowed for more time with their families or even relocated to rural areas.

The pandemic has also brought mental health to the forefront of societal discussions. The collective experience of isolation and uncertainty has prompted a more open dialogue about mental well-being and the importance of seeking support when needed. As a result, there has been a greater societal emphasis on emotional health and self-care."

Superstitions in Business

Business is not exempt from superstition. Business rituals and ceremonies can be deeply influenced by superstitions. These rituals, often incorporating elements of purification and blessings, are performed to ward off negative energy and attract good fortune. The principles of Feng Shui, which focus on the flow of energy and balance in a space, are often applied to office design. Companies may consult Feng Shui experts to optimise their office design and layout to promote harmony, productivity, and success. In some regions, businesses pay careful attention to the opening and closing timing. Superstitions related to celestial events, lunar phases, or astrological alignments can affect decisions about when to start or end the business day.

Meeting Etiquette

As is commonly known, handling visiting cards has a unique procedure in business. Visiting cards are considered an extension of a person's identity and are given much respect. There are meticulous rules around how they should be carried, handled, and stored. People do not keep them in their wallets, as wallets are usually kept in the back pocket. Cards are always placed in front of the person receiving them on the meeting table, in a clean row, and in such a way that they're easily readable throughout the meeting, helping the recipient recall other people's titles and hierarchy. Breaking these norms is considered impolite and is perhaps never done. When going to a business meeting, event, or party, it's inappropriate not to carry your card. It happened to me once, and I recall how embarrassed I felt telling people each time they gave me their card that I was not carrying my card.

In business meetings, the practice is to wait to be seated in a meeting room because there are norms regarding who sits where and on which side of the table. No derogatory remarks are made about anyone, including competitors or one's own employees. Business preparedness is highly desired, and people will ask many questions, expecting the answers to be available. It is expected that a lot of notes be taken since it indicates a person's interest in the subject. Local people, in turn, are trained to take notes.

They say that when a meeting is over, the meeting continues! Very often, meetings move to restaurants or bars. The vibe is completely different. Food and alcohol are used as a social lubricant and are a way to connect with the person. People will not be judged much during such events, but it's a chance to make oneself more likable, and it's okay to unwind and be casual.

After dinner and drinks, one of the favourite pastimes is karaoke. One can be an awesome singer or an awful one, and no one will actually care or pay attention to it. It's all about unwinding a little and bonding together[36].

Quality and Efficiency in Business

Multinational companies regularly introduce new products in global markets. They announce and roll out the new product. However, in Japan, products sometimes go through additional quality and customer convenience checks before being launched. In the company I worked for, I remember instances of new products that already had a low failure rate during testing in the global factories being reworked in the ir local Japan factory to further reduce the failure rate before being shipped to customers. A globally accepted failure rate was not good enough for the Japanese. During my stay there, I witnessed an instance where a multinational company sold one of its businesses to a Chinese company, and the sales of that product immediately dropped in Japan. In other countries, when ownership changed, buyer behaviour did not change much. However, the Japanese somehow wanted to be cautious about a likely drop in quality standards and watched the market reports on the quality of the products produced by the Chinese company before recommencing buying.

As you would expect by now, quality and efficiency are paramount in the world of business. Pioneering practices like LEAN have become the gold standard worldwide. Precision and strict compliance with procedures are what have made their famed business practice 'kanban' or 'Just-in-Time' manufacturing possible, resulting in huge efficiency and productivity.

Here are two examples of efficiency in businesses and at work. At the office, when my secretary would take leave, she would make sure that the stand-in secretary was fully briefed about my working style and all aspects of support required by me, including details of all my meetings, calls, and any follow-up work that was required that day(s). I did not have to spend any time bringing the stand-in person up to speed or providing direction. No time was lost despite her being new to that role.

The topic of excellence in cost management will invariably remind us of the Japanese and their way of managing it. Stories of focus on the cost and efficiency of Japanese companies, especially around the 80s and 90s, are legendary and will remain case studies for a long time. One of the management tools they use is called Genchi Genbutsu, i.e., going to a place to see the actual situation to gain a better understanding. In pursuit of optimising costs and improving quality, a reputed automobile manufacturer asked its highly qualified engineers at mid and senior levels, who worked mostly out of corporate head offices, to spend time on the factory shop floor where manufacturing and engineering work actually takes place. They transferred some of them to their factory for a year (instead of sending them on one or two weeks of fact-finding missions). The skilled senior officers closely observed each factory floor operation and process — material ordering, storage and movement, time and inventory management, and product design. They identified several inefficiencies and recommended process improvements in design, production, inventory, and logistics that achieved the twin objectives of improving quality and lowering cost. What they did was simple: observed, hands-on, how and where cost was being incurred.

Process and Procedure

As a culture, the business processes and procedures laid out are strictly followed. If a person feels that a certain procedure is wrong or inefficient, he/she will follow it meticulously and not break it. If a person wishes to change a procedure, he/she will need to involve the right stakeholders and go through detailed steps such as discussing the pros and cons in detail, thinking through all its implications, preparing the revised procedure, communicating it, and training people if required. Only after all these aspects are taken care of would it be implemented. Not that other countries don't do many of these, but in Japan, they go into great detail, and the rules of changing anything apply, somewhat annoyingly, in the same manner to small things as they would for more important matters.

The principle behind the high focus on procedure is that for something to work perfectly, all you have to do is follow a process and you will get the desired result (the legendary Indian Cricket captain M S Dhoni frequently quotes this philosophy when he says "focus on the process and results will follow"). The culture is not just about doing something but about doing it the right way. We've heard of the phrase 'method in the madness'. In Japan, it is 'madness about the method'!

Politeness and Respect

In business, high respect is shown towards individuals in senior **positions**, those senior in age, and those formerly in senior positions. As a matter of business etiquette, **people are** expected to hold emotions in check, even among peers, and confrontations and emotional expressions within and outside the organisation **are** avoided. Foreigners dealing with them are advised to avoid a hard-sell, high-pressure approach since pushing hard on decisions and deadlines is inconsistent with their consensus-based decision-making. Instead, business is **conducted** through persuasion, relationships, and trust. Major conflicts are dealt with indirectly through an intermediary or informally – for **example**, as part of after-office-hours socialising.

At the company I worked for, in dealing with the Japanese, the U.S parent company used a different approach compared to other countries. While the US HQ expected absolute compliance with all policies and procedures from every country in which they operated, both the U.S. and the Asia-Pacific HQ were very sensitive to Japanese culture, preferences, and style. They were allowed more leeway in changing things according to their needs and local practices. Many policies were implemented after discussion rather than through dictat. The unwritten norm was to treat them almost with kid gloves without pushing them around. This approach of according special treatment to them was more out of a grudging realisation that asking them to deviate from their preferred ways would be counter-productive because they would, in any case, do things only their way.

Of course, politeness comes in different ways in different cultures. In the global corporate world, we hear some rather routine thanking of people. We've all heard these expressions:

Thank you for your mail.

Thank you in advance.

Thank you for asking the question.

Thank you for joining the call.

Thank you for inviting me to the call.

Like a "thank you" factory.

Once, after the annual sports day at the American school, we received a letter saying, "Dear parents, we would like to thank you for sharing your child with the school to participate in the sports day event"! Pray… why should a school thank parents for this, and what exactly is "sharing your child"? I know it is harmless, but it is funny. Courtesy seems a bit meaningless sometimes. For instance in office, every question asked during a question-and-answer session (Q&A) will be followed by an "Oh, that's a great question." One wonders how every single question, asked by every single person, in every meeting is a GREAT question. Someday someone is going to raise their hand and say:

"Can I ask a question?"

….and the reply will be

"Oh, that's a great question."

Business and Societal Challenges

(some minor, some major)

Working with the Japanese has its own challenges. Their emotions are always in check, and they are hence hard to read. If someone answers a difficult question or proposal with a yes, it does not signify agreement, but may merely mean that they understand. Some of it can be peculiar. In our company, we once had a business problem, and in the opinion of the Asia-Pacific headquarters, to which Japan reported, it was caused by a goof-up by the Japanese team. A furious senior Asia HQ executive called them for a review meeting. Anticipating an angry boss, the Japanese manager came to the meeting along with 18 other team members and a 67-page presentation. It is very difficult to have a tough discussion with so many people in the room. Was that the idea of bringing a big team along? Passive aggression?

When working with them, it appears, it is very hard for a foreigner to obtain their trust. But once a person has demonstrated loyalty to the organisation and they become very comfortable with a person, from being very hesitant and cautious, they become extremely trusting and empowering.

Some of these relatively smaller issues apart, the larger issue for Japanese society is that they are no longer perceived as the leaders in innovation. Their business and industry are no longer creating a Toyota, Sony, or Mitsubishi. The explanation I recently received for this is that (and I quote), "In a fast-changing and globalised world, agility and risk-taking have become even more important, requiring a different mindset to navigate the ever-changing tech landscape. The local corporate culture there traditionally values stability and incremental improvement and this. The cultural preference for stability and risk aversion has often overshadowed the spirit of innovation.

Emerging markets have different demands and tastes, and addressing these shifting preferences requires a deep understanding of local markets and consumer behaviour, something the Japanese companies have not been able to keep pace with when compared with their American counterparts."

I agreed with him. One has to admire America's culture of innovation and the ability to create global corporations at high-speed and agility. On the obvious significance of risk-taking in business, I once asked my nephew, who had then migrated to the USA and spent a few years there, as to what makes America so great in innovation and business? I thought his three-word reply, "They accept failure." was well put. This is true of American society and the business community. Business failure is not looked down upon by society or key investors like venture funds. To investors, it's the business idea that matters along with the person's track record. This has, I am sure, been a big factor in America converting ideas into innovation and business success. It is this aspect of risk-taking and the importance of not losing face in society that perhaps slows down business growth.

What the Japanese have to Say about Indians

Having discussed the experiences of living there, I wanted to share a quick perspective on what the Japanese perceive about living and working in India. It will be a very brief account and is not intended to be comprehensive. A friend of mine has been working for a Japanese company in Bangalore for many years and was a good source of information for me. I asked him about their working style and what they like and do not like about India.

What they like about India is people's capability in general, our technical and engineering skills, our flexibility, and hard work. They admire the skill of Indians in crisis management. Interestingly, they have also come to appreciate our Jugaad innovation. Wow, that's something, given all that we have read so far about their obsession with high-quality.

What they do not like about dealing with Indians is our complete disrespect for punctuality and the habit of being vague on promises made like - "do minute mein ho jayega" (it will be done in two minutes), when we almost surely know it will take half an hour or more. We will say "Abhi das minute mein aa raha hoon" (I will be there in just 10 minutes) and show up one hour later. About Indians, they also think that we sometimes talk too much and, of course, hate the traffic.

It appears when it is time for them to go back home after their assignment in India, many of them do not like the idea of returning. They love all the domestic help available in India in the form of maid, driver, or gardener and dislike the idea of having to do it all by themselves when they return home.

A Japanese national shared his view too. I quote: "India is a dynamic blend of spirituality and practicality. India's rich spiritual culture, steeped in traditions, has given rise to a unique and profound mindset among its people. What truly fascinates me is the way this mindset seamlessly encompasses both spiritual depth and a seemingly contradictory sense of realism, practicality, and highly logical thinking. It's a captivating dynamism that I have come to admire. There is also a genuine acceptance and celebration of diversity, which sets it apart and holds great significance in a global context.

It reflects a fundamental and truthful way of viewing the world as one interconnected global community".

"One thing that resonates deeply with us is the authenticity of people and human interaction. People here often express their emotions openly, whether through moments of shyness, heartfelt encounters, or exuberant expressions of joy, sometimes involving dancing or using their entire body to convey their feelings. There's a profound sense of being in touch with one's humanity, a genuine authenticity that I find incredibly appealing. It's as if the essence of what it means to be human is vividly alive here, and I cherish this aspect greatly".

Nice words, I thought.

Chapter 6

EXITING TOKYO

As I mentioned earlier, IBM relocated its Asia-Pacific headquarters from Tokyo to Shanghai. After considering options, I decided to be part of this move and go to Shanghai versus returning to India. It was one of the more difficult decisions I had to make, as we had already relocated twice in the past three years, from Bangalore to Singapore to Tokyo and now once again, this time to Shanghai. The choice of where to go from Tokyo became more important as the boys were now older, and education scenarios carried high weightage, making the decision process lengthy and stressful.

As expected, our experiences in the two years we lived there were varied, a mixed bag of more good, some funny, and some very difficult times. It was a country where watermelons are cube-shaped, not round, a very safe country where we faced burglary, one where the deepest underground train station is over 200 feet below ground level, literally in 'pataal lok,' and a society that's experiencing high post-retirement divorces. When it was time to leave the country, none of us in the family liked the idea. There was so much we saw and experienced that weighed very favourably in our minds when we left.

I think Japanese society is the most unique in the world. As we interact with or travel to different countries, we always observe differences in people and culture. Yet many aspects of behaviour remain common across countries - what we often describe as basic human nature. The Japanese, however, are unique in many ways - nothing exemplifying this more than the example of the 2011 Tsunami that I described earlier.

Two years in Tokyo flew by, and we had to pack and move. The packing process had its share of irritation. When the packers came in, they insisted that we fill in the value of each and every item being shipped. So, we were asked to assign a separate value to each item in a bed i.e., the value of wood, of the mattress, and of bed linen. They said that that is how insurance worked. It was a ridiculous exercise. We started off doing it seriously, but got tired very quickly and filled up random values just for the sake of it.

Every time we relocated countries, both before we occupied the new house, and after we had emptied all furniture at the time of leaving, there was a tradition among the three male members in our family - play a game of Cricket in the living room. How typically Indian. Japan was certainly not a place to break tradition. So, we didn't and played Cricket for almost an hour. My wife would keep reminding us to stop playing and leave, but, like little children, we kept saying "5 more minutes," "5 more minutes," buying more time, reflecting the underlying reluctance to leave the home and the country.

On our way out, at the airport, we purchased another Harry Potter book, which brought a few smiles to the otherwise sullen faces of the two boys. It was time to board the 11.25 a.m JAL flight… and to say… Sayonara.

China

Chapter 7

OUR STAY AND EXPERIENCES

Chinna chinna aasai ....

Have I wrongly spelled China as Chinna? Well, not really. I am referring to the mega-hit music composition by A. R. Rahman from the epic Tamil movie ROJA that was playing in the restaurant, the Indian Kitchen, where we went for our very first meal in Shanghai. (The song goes as "Dil hai chota sa, choti si asha" in Hindi). The Chinese male waiters in the restaurant were wearing pyjama-kurta, and women wore a bindi (red dot on the forehead) and a half-sari. To add to these settings, there was a huge statue of Shiva at the restaurant entrance. It was a pleasant welcome in communist land. Familiarity is certainly soothing.

We had moved into a country which until the 1980s was fairly isolated from the world. A country that was a mystery to many and seemed an unlikely place for foreigners to travel, let alone live in. A historic land of great inventions like paper, silk, tea, compass, clock, porcelain and one that houses the colossal 21,000 km long Great Wall, built over a span of 1800 years. A nation that has, perhaps, faced more loss of human lives due to wars and natural disasters than any other (Annexure 2). And yes, a country whose one tiny area in Tibet is Mount Kailash (Lord Shiva's abode), that Hindus have a special place for in their heart.

Upon landing in Shanghai, our ride from the airport to the city was by a taxi. There is one other high-tech option to get to the city – by the 'flying' train – Maglev, but we had too much luggage to opt for a train ride. The Maglev train was built in 2001, in less than 2 years, it covers the distance of 29 km, from the Shanghai airport to the city, in 8 minutes travelling at a peak speed of 431 km per hour. The Maglev technology uses magnetic levitation, rather than wheels on rails, and makes no contact with the ground. So, in a sense it flies just above the ground. Magnets provide the propulsion, and the absence of any friction with the rails enables such high speeds. The magnetic fields counteract gravity. It is to date the fastest commercial train in the world.

Our First Month in Shanghai

The city of Shanghai (meaning "above-the-sea"), where we lived, is located along the Yangtze River delta, as of 2022 has a population of ~29 million people and is a symbol of modern China. Geographically, the city is divided into two large areas - called Puxi (x is pronounced as "sh", so it's Pu-shi) and Pudong, that are on either side of the Huang Pu River. In the 90s Pudong was a marshy area with agricultural fields, but 15 years later, it was a bustling city over 40 kms long – a lot like how Gurugram has developed since the early 2000s. It possibly has the maximum number of international schools (over 40) in any city in the world.

A few months before we arrived, we travelled to Shanghai for a look-see trip, mainly to identify a house and obtain school admissions. Unlike when we moved in prior years, to Singapore and Tokyo, my two sons accompanied my wife and me during this trip - a new experience for them. They had grown up enough to provide inputs on house selection and, unhappy as they were about the need to move again, it helped them feel more part of the new city and life. There are several truly international schools there, unlike some in India that simply carry the suffix International in their names, yet resemble them mainly in high fees, not in the quality of faculty or student mix.

On day one of the look-see trip, the real-estate agent, RY, showed us a list of 6 apartments that she'd take us to. I protested – "What? Just 6? I need to see more." After all, we seen more than a dozen in Tokyo (somewhere perhaps was the fear of completing all work within 2 days and returning home. You see, I was on a paid holiday for 1 week). RY said, "Ok I will show you 12. But you will finally select building X or building Y from the original list of 6. Your company employees prefer only these buildings." Like ghettos, I suppose. And sure enough, after seeing more apartments, we selected one from the two she had originally suggested.

When we finally moved into the city a month later, RY helped us with initial formalities. For expatriates, in most countries, house lease contracts are signed between the landlord and the company. But the company I worked had a practice, in China, of asking the employee to enter into a lease contract directly with the landlord. The problem was that agreements were in Mandarin. I was uneasy signing on a document which I did not understand a word of, but somewhat laughed off the nervousness by reminding myself that as Indians, it is common for us to sign documents in a language we just do not understand. We sign documents that are in Bengali, Marathi, or Kannada, of which we have no clue.

You have to permit me to brag about our apartment. It was in a gated community of seven 66-storey buildings along the Huang Pu River. The apartment complex had a very fancy, massive clubhouse, a park, a fine-dining, Chinese restaurant. It had two swimming pools, including a heated one, a separate wave pool with an artificial 'beach' and an artificial lake with a dozen swans. The living room in our apartment had a huge glass wall – from ceiling to floor and up to both ends of the room. We had a fantastic view of the adjoining river and of the 'beach' in our compound. Aur kya chahiye? (What else do you need?). Good enough to show off to guests. Well…., that was until a cyclonic storm came a few weeks later. The already high wind speed was worsened by the river being adjacent to the apartment. The sealant holding the glass wall in place began to come off, and it started rattling. After a while, it looked like the glass would shatter, exposing us fully to nature's fury. It was scary. It would have made the living room one of a kind – one side open to nature. The storm shook the glass and us. We stopped bragging to our friends.

The first evening after we moved in, we went to a nearby local Chinese department store. We got the grocery items we looked for, but the aisles of the store were filled with live seafood. All kinds of sea creatures floating in tubs – crabs, eel, fish, et al. The local people would buy them, get them chopped, and take them home. Not used to this, my pure vegetarian wife squealed – "where the hell have you brought me? I am not going to live in this country." A decision we made that day, to go only to bigger, international stores, rather than the local ones, subsided the crisis.

Two weeks after moving in, I decided to get a hair re-engineering (cutting and colouring) done. The club-house in our gated community had a nice barber shop. I went there and asked for this service. After a haircut, when the hairdresser began mixing the hair colour, I noticed that it was a famous brand. Since China has a lot of fake products, I asked her, "Is that *real?*". She said, "Yes, it is *L'Oreal!*" She looked confused as I laughed at her reply and at myself.

Priorities in a New Country

The first few months are about getting a condensed course on what can go right or wrong and make you angry or laugh. Having lived on foreign soil, by now, we had a fair idea of what to expect. It does help that, in most cities in the world, there are a good number of Indians, and making friends quickly provides early comfort.

For those who may not have moved countries, let me list some of the important things that must get done in the first few weeks and months.

Among the first things one needs in a new country is a work permit. Obtaining it was a fairly smooth process and took about two weeks. When the work permit was under process, I was asked to travel to Seoul, Korea for a meeting. So I filled the visa application, gave it to my secretary, and told her that when the passport would come back from the Chinese government with a work permit, she should send it to the Korean embassy along with the form to obtain a visa. She filled the Korean visa form, I signed it and left it with her. Since I had just arrived in the country, there was enough to do at the office and home, and I forgot about the Korean visa matter. A few days before the trip, I asked her if the visa had been obtained. She said "yes". I looked through the passport but could not find the Korean visa and asked her why it was not obtained. She said that she did not apply for a Korean visa, but I could go ahead and travel to Seoul since China had already given me a work permit for 2 years. I could enter China anytime I wanted during this period and so, she thought that there was no need for a Korean visa! Hmmm... she was obviously under-exposed to visa matters. Wish she had checked with me. It was too late by then to apply for a visa, and I could not travel for the meeting.

You have to retune your head to convert the local currency to Rupees, quickly learn a few words in the local language that can get you home in an emergency, and make enough new friends to feel comfortable. In the course of time, the mix of friends you make in the new country must have enough 'goras' (foreigners i.e., non-Indians) in such a way that when the number of non-Indian friends is multiplied by 5 to exaggerate, you could appear sufficiently global and cool.

One needs to learn a few basic words in the local language as quickly as possible. Very few people speak English in China. To commute within the city, we always had to print the address, print a map, or show a hotel's business card. The peculiar thing about China is that though popular locations had an English name, they all had a corresponding Mandarin name as well. For example, to take a taxi when returning home, instead of saying our building name "Shimao Riviera Garden," we had to say the Mandarin equivalent "Shimao Bin Jiang Huao Yuan." Taxi drivers and locals would only understand the Mandarin name. To ease the language problem for expatriates, IBM allowed secretarial assistants to act as translators and help in getting personal work done too. So, for interactions with a plumber, carpenter, or driver, we could ask the secretary for help. This was very useful.

When in a new country, there is, of course, a great temptation to constantly compare the host country with India. Which one is better is sometimes fact-based, sometimes a matter of convenience. For example, at the office, the right thing to do is to complain to your boss about how difficult it is for your family to live in the country you are in and what a huge sacrifice you are making for the company. The frequency and intensity of the complaint would depend on how close the annual increment date is. Your boss will not like it, may even curse you in his/her mind, but that's ok. Because he/she will be complaining to his/her boss about their own family's difficulties in the foreign country and the immense sacrifices they are making for the company.

In the new city, 'life-support' has to be purchased, i.e., an Indian cable TV connection. And here's a funny incident that happened when we tried to 'decorate' our house with it. We found an agent who would give us Indian TV channels. Once again, the options were limited – as in Japan, they were mainly Sahara channels. A week after installation, the agent came home unannounced, along with another Chinese guy. They seemed to get into some intense discussion and, within a few minutes, the two men started arguing loudly in Mandarin, making my wife very uncomfortable. To figure out the problem, she pressed the emergency button, i.e., called my secretary for language support. After speaking with the cable TV guys at home, she explained that the reason for the fight was that, while providing us the TV connection, our agent did not use a new cable but instead tapped an existing cable line already installed by the other cable operator in the building, a few floors above ours. The other guy was naturally furious. In their fight, they nearly came to blows. But, even as my wife, rather helplessly, watched the fight, the two guys suddenly started laughing and hugging. The secret of this dramatic change in the scenario was that during their heated verbal exchange, they found that they were from the same gaon (village). Suddenly, all was well, and stealing a cable connection was no longer an issue. They just walked away from home without conversing a single word with my wife throughout the 20 odd minutes of drama.

Humorous Enthusiasm

Foreigners in China usually lease a car along with an English-speaking driver instead of buying one because of potential language issues in dealing with the police or the locals. We did the same thing – leased a car. Within a few months of hiring a car and driver, we observed that our driver was asking for money to fill petrol rather frequently, and a simple tracking of mileage made us realise that he was stealing petrol. I complained to the car leasing company about it. They said that they would speak to the driver and assured me that it wouldn't happen again. But, after an initial pause for some weeks, the driver started stealing again. I then asked my assistant in the office to inform the car leasing company to replace the driver and said that if they did not agree, I would have to cancel the lease. She called and informed the car hire company. The events that ensued in the next few hours were frustrating and hilarious.

My wife had to go to a few places for shopping that morning – the usual errands. After some shopping at smaller stores, she went into a mall. After over an hour, she came out and called the driver, asking him to pick her up. He told her something angrily in Mandarin and disconnected the phone. All she understood from what he said was my secretary's name, and so she called her to enquire. My secretary said: "It is not right for a driver to cheat a foreigner like you. It is shameful for my country. I asked the leasing company to take immediate action against the driver since he was cheating you, and to provide you another driver. It appears they told the driver that he will be removed from service. He fought with them and quit his job on the spot. He has refused to drive any further." The driver, who had literally abandoned my wife on the street, came to my office in the car and handed over all the purchases made earlier to my secretary. She had no choice but to bring it up to the office and, since her workstation was small, she left it on my desk. I was in a meeting and had no idea of what was going on. When I came back to my desk, to my shock, I noticed vegetables, kitchenware, a painting, and some assorted items lying on my table. My wife took a taxi and came home, completely frustrated and fuming.

The agency called me and told me that they were short of drivers and the only driver available was a lady. I saw no reason why a lady should not be hired for the job and asked them to go ahead and appoint her. It did create some humour in the office, as even the Europeans and Americans used to, jokingly, make fun of me for having a lady driver.

Our driver called me one day in the morning and said, "My father had a heart attack. I will be half an hour late." Sounded funny. If one's father had an attack, one should be spending more than 30 minutes taking care of the situation. It transpired that she was not telling me the truth. In China, as in India, helpers usually tell big lies when they are late for work or want to take a day or two off. In India, for example, the maid servants will announce that her grandmother had passed away and she needed leave. Over time, if one added up, 3-4 grandmothers would have passed away☺. They say such things because, quite often, the employer will express unhappiness when asked leave, and so the helpers cook up such drastic stories. I suppose the employers are to blame.

A *Broken* Plane

Another anxious and amusing incident happened with our family during a holiday travel some months later. China has three holiday breaks in a year, and all three are one week long - Chinese New Year (based on the lunar calendar), Labour Week (May 1-7), and National Week (Oct 1-7). Since they do not have many religious holidays, it perhaps is planned that way to promote commerce, resulting in millions travelling across the country back to their homes or to a holiday destination. During one such holiday, we went to Xian (pronounced "Shi-an"), to see the famed terracotta warrior museum.

The museum is a collection of terracotta sculptures depicting the armies of Qin Shi Huang, the first Emperor of China. It is a form of funerary art where the sculptures are buried with the emperor to protect the emperor in his afterlife. The figures, dating from 210–209 BCE, were discovered in 1974 by local farmers in Lintong District, Xi'an, in the Shaanxi province. Four main pits, each approximately 7 metres (23 ft.) deep, were excavated. It is estimated that the three pits containing the terracotta army held more than 8,000 soldiers, 130 chariots with 520 horses and 150 cavalry horses, the majority of which remained buried in the pits nearby Qin Shi Huang's mausoleum. The sculptures varied in height according to the roles of each category of people depicted, with the tallest being that of the generals. Non-military figures were also found in other pits, including officials, acrobats, strongmen, and musicians[37].

The drama began when we reached the airport for our return flight to Shanghai. The four of us checked in and sat near the gate at the departure lounge, awaiting a boarding announcement. There was some announcement in Mandarin, and suddenly, all the passengers seated around us started walking away from the gate. We didn't know the reason since the flight schedule monitor showed something in Mandarin. We then asked an airline staff, who was hurrying past us, what the matter was. He said "broken". We asked, "What is broken?" And he replied "Airplane." We interpreted it that the aircraft had a technical snag and that we had to wait for it to be repaired, or for another aircraft. The airline staff then gestured to us to follow him. We followed him, and the noise in his walkie-talkie, walking a pretty long distance before exiting the terminal. He then gestured us to wait. He knew no English and couldn't tell us what was happening.

After maybe 20 minutes, a bus arrived. He pointed to the door. Like faithful pets, we boarded it without any idea where it would take us. It was already about 7 p.m and dark. The bus drove about 15 mins. The few others in the bus were all locals, so all we could do was guess that it would lead to a hotel, which it did. Everyone got down, so we too stepped out. They all walked into the hotel lobby. Like them, we showed the hotel staff our boarding pass and they asked us to join a queue. After a wait, the reception staff gave us two room keys. Again, no English, no communication of how long we would have to stay there. Was it a few hours? Was it overnight? Unfortunately, that day we were unable to contact my secretary for translation, as she too was on vacation somewhere, and so, we bided time restlessly in the room.

After five hours, which seemed like twenty-five, around maybe 1.30 am in the night, we heard some noise in the aisle of our hotel floor. The children were asleep and my wife and I half-asleep. Hearing the noise, we opened the door and saw many people walk briskly. We quickly pulled out our boarding pass and showed it to them, asking if they were leaving for that flight. We got a yes head-shake in reply and some words in Mandarin which we did not understand. The four of us picked up our bags and rushed to the lobby, re-confirmed that we were headed to the airport, and got to a waiting bus. We reached the airport and the correct boarding gate. Fortunately, the gate mentioned our flight number. We boarded the plane and took off. A very crazy experience. Just two words in English - broken plane, to guide us through about 7+ hours in an alien land. What a nice way to end a vacation.

East vs West: An Incident Revealing Complementing Cultures

An incident occurred in the office that brought out contrasting and complementary behaviour among colleagues. A colleague in my team from India had diabetes. One afternoon, he was so engrossed with work that he kept working well past lunchtime, forgetting to have his meal. To maintain sugar levels, people with diabetes are expected to eat on time and, in fact, have small bites of food frequently—a rule this colleague forgot. His blood sugar level dropped, and he suddenly collapsed onto the floor and fainted. Others around him took immediate action, called for an ambulance, and rushed him to the hospital. He was treated, recovered quickly, spent a day there, and then was discharged. As all of this was happening, I witnessed how two cultures—the West and the East—had different yet complementary priorities and responses. Once he was admitted to the hospital, the Westerners in the office were very concerned about issues like the time taken for the ambulance to arrive, the ease of getting immediate medical care at the hospital, the availability of first aid kits in the office, and how quickly his family was informed. The Asians made arrangements for his wife to be picked up and brought to the hospital, discussed with her the help she needed in taking care of their 8-month-old baby, and worried about what led to the employee skipping a meal that caused the fainting. The Westerners worried about the process to handle such situations in the office, while the Indians and other Asians were concerned about the softer emotional support to the family. Both groups asked all the relevant questions and did all the important things, yet their priorities were different, and fortunately, complementary.

China's Visible Infrastructure and Development

From the time we first landed in Shanghai, we could see signs of modern, high-quality infrastructure. In the Pudong area of Shanghai, close to where we lived, in the space of 5-6 years, three very tall skyscrapers were built: the 88-storey Jin Mao towers for hotels and offices, the 105-storey World Financial Centre, and the 128-storey Shanghai Tower. Both the 100+ storey buildings were adjacent to my office and were built after I moved to Shanghai, allowing me the opportunity to witness the great speed with which they were built in a short time period of about 4 years, using state-of-the-art technology. It felt like a new floor came up every week.

Urban planning was fabulous and is exemplified by the urban planning museum in Shanghai. The entire Shanghai metropolitan area—i.e., every single street and building, both current and planned over the following 20 years—was represented by way of a miniature model in the museum.

To build good infrastructure, land acquisition is the first big task. Historically, the government owned all land in the country. Private land ownership was allowed around the 1990s. The local municipality could take over a piece of land or building for development. They would intimate its owners/tenants of this decision and allot alternate space or pay monetary compensation. We got a glimpse of one such acquisition. Just two roads away from our own apartment, when we tried going to a shop that we had been to two months earlier, we could not locate it. An entire row of buildings had been razed down, and a new road built there. The shop had vanished. So much for using shops and buildings as landmarks while locating places.

The Largest Infrastructure Project

One of the largest projects of infrastructure development in China is the Three Gorges Dam spanning a 700 km stretch along the Yangtze River. It was constructed to create a large power station (the world's largest, in fact), increase shipping capacity, and reduce downstream floods. The river level was raised across the long stretch, in many cases by over 10 times. The dam took 10 years to build and impacted the lives of 1.3 million people who lived in that route and had to relocate.

Our own personal experience of the Three Gorges Dam project was by way of a cruise along the river and the dam site. Throughout the journey, we saw towns relocated and new towns built. Crossing the ship lock (see picture) at the dam site was a memorable experience for us. For those not familiar with a ship lock, it is a structure built to facilitate ships and boats to travel up or down stream rivers and canals. The height of the Three Gorges Dam is 607 feet, and ships and boats use the ship lock to ascend or descend this height. It has four levels or 'steps' with walls on two sides and huge 16-tonne gates in front and behind. When a ship has to go downstream, it first enters step 1. The gates behind it then close, thereby 'locking' the ship in its place. Once locked, the water beneath the ship is very slowly drained out, bringing the ship to the same level as the next step below. The front gate is then opened for the ship to move to the next step, where the locking and water-draining process gets repeated. This is how the ship or boat is able to go down the river at the dam site. This entire process takes about three hours, and it was quite an experience. Apart from the ship lock, at this site, an elevator was being built to carry very small boats up and down to save time! In our trip, this process began at 1 am, and we stayed up that night until 4 am to experience passing through the ship lock.

Great Use of Rivers

The river adjoining our apartment, Huang Pu, that bisects Shanghai, presented a fine example of China making excellent use of its waterways for transportation. Large and medium-sized ships, including ocean-liners, constantly traversed it, carrying heavy commodities like coal, steel, cement, sand, and cars, helping reduce transportation costs and pollution from using trucks. Across the country, the government invested heavily in making rivers navigable. India, despite having 7,500 km of coastline all along Eastern, Southern, and Western India and lots of rivers (including some that have water in them ☺), has not been able to leverage this natural resource well for transportation.

Chapter 8

SOCIETY, CUSTOMS, TRADITION

Along with Egypt, modern-day Iraq, India, Peru, and Mexico, China is one of the six oldest civilisations in the world. Protected by the Himalayan Mountains, Pacific Ocean, and Gobi Desert and situated between the Yellow and Yangtze rivers, the earliest Chinese civilisations flourished in isolation from invaders and other foreigners for centuries. Like the Egyptians, the ancient Chinese were able to mobilise populations to build massive infrastructure projects, including, of course, the Great Wall of China (built around 220 BCE to stop Mongol invaders) and the 5th-century-era Grand Canal, which links the Yellow and Yangtze rivers, allowing vast numbers of military forces and goods to move across the country[38].

The Chinese civilisation is credited with developing the decimal system, abacus, and sundial, as well as the printing press, which allowed for the publication and distribution of Sun Tzu's The Art of War, still relevant more than 2,500 years later. Other famous inventions include paper (105 B.C), silk (~6000 years ago), tea, alcohol (~ 2000 years ago), gunpowder (~ 2000 years ago), clock (725 A.D), compass (~ 1100 A.D), iron smelting, porcelain (600 A.D), acupuncture (~2000 years ago), and anaesthesia, bronze (1700 B.C, used to make weapons & tools), and kite (1000 B.C).[39] There are varying information on who invented alcohol. One version says it was the Arabs, not the Chinese. But Indians may argue that ancient Indian texts, many thousand years old, make distinct reference to *Madhu*. So was it invented in India? It's not very clear. Alcohol, after all, is bound to generate a debate.

As expected from a country so ancient and large, China has varying cultural practices depending on geography and ethnicity, with about 60 ethnic and minority groups (India apparently has 2,000+ ethnic groups). China is a much more homogeneous society, having a common culture across the country, with the largest community, the Han Chinese, being a 91% majority ethnic group. Labour force participation among women is 61% (i.e., 61% of women above 15 years are employed), compared with India's 24%[40]. Yet the representation of women in politics is low, in fact, lower than in India.

The societal culture, especially as it relates to the home and family, is similar to India's in aspects of family orientation, the importance of face-saving, superstition, respect for elders, and rituals for ancestors. At home and in business, China is a closely-knit society. Among the Chinese, family orientation is strong, as emphasised by Confucian philosophy of filial piety. The pride or pain of the individual is the pride or pain of the family. Face-saving in the society is a very important personal trait. Their reputation and that of the family need careful guarding, have to be maintained at all costs, and losing it would amount to humiliation.

I will now move on to talk about their:

- Language

- Superstition and beliefs

- Religion and

- Food

Language and Language Goof-Ups

The Chinese language does not have alphabets. Instead, there is a system of characters that represent ideas and sounds. Altogether there are over 50,000 characters, though a comprehensive modern dictionary will rarely list over 20,000 in use. An educated Chinese person will know about 8,000 characters, but you will need about 2-3,000 to be able to read a newspaper[41]. There is logic around the strokes in a character that makes it easier for people to remember. Each character can have as many as 30 strokes, and all varieties of spoken Chinese are tonal. This means that each syllable can have a number of different meanings depending on the tone with which it is pronounced. Mandarin has 4 tones, and Cantonese has between 6 and 9[42]. In using words, the context is very important. Even one different stroke within 10 or 20 that make the character gives it a totally different meaning.

The script appears complex.

"What's your name?" is written as

「叫什「名字?

"Please keep your goods safely" is written as

「妥善保管「的「物.

Some characters reflect their meaning in a quite literal sense. For example, the word for "China" is "Zhōngguó".

The characters that represent this word illustrate how Chinese people viewed China as being at the centre of the world – literally a middle kingdom[43].

There is no gender differentiator. He and she are used interchangeably. In the office, I have heard this sentence: "If you see Charles, tell her to meet me."

English Language Blues

Since English is not their first language, they are challenged in its usage. The extent can be gauged by very funny English language signboards in the pictures attached[44]. (They are real—no photoshop involved. There are several websites on funny signboards in China.)

Language Goof-ups by Foreigners

Stories of foreigners goofing up the local language and embarrassing themselves are universal. We and our friends were no exception. Here are some:

An Australian friend of ours had this funny incident to tell us. She had completed about four months of Mandarin classes. She once boarded a taxi and instead of sitting on the rear seat, she chose to sit in the front seat, next to the cab driver, as she wanted to converse with him and practice Mandarin. As she sat down, she told him where she wanted to go. The driver got very upset and started saying, "No, no, no, I am a married man. I even have a child." She was totally confused, wondering why on earth was he telling her that he's a married man? Only after a few seconds did she realise that instead of telling him "Take me to this hotel", she asked him "Will you come with me to a hotel?" The fact that she chose to sit next to him, and not in the rear seat, made the driver even more suspicious. She vowed to experiment less with the language.

Within a few weeks of their arrival in China, the local maid at our close friend's house told her in Mandarin that she would "Clean their tappaloosi another day." Our friend nodded in acceptance but was delighted at learning a new Mandarin word; i.e., that the word for toilet in Mandarin was "Tappaloosi." Only to realise later that "tappaloosi" was nothing else but their maid's Chinese way of pronouncing WC! Amusing. The same word, with the same meaning, was being used by one person as English and by another as Mandarin.

My own Mandarin vocabulary was no more than a few words. But bravery has always been a human virtue. We had gone to a restaurant for lunch. Mid-way through it, the waitress inquired how the food was. Instead of saying "It is very nice," I said "You are very nice." My wife, who knew more Mandarin, let out that **unmatched** South Indian expression ayyo. Fortunately for me, we were in public, and so, she slapped her forehead, not me.

Language Fees

One evening, while playing with his friends within the building, my 11-year-old son fell down, bruised his knees, and was bleeding slightly—a pretty common occurrence in all our lives. Some of the adults around him inquired about his door number. He told them that his mother had gone out and his father was in the office. He gave them my mobile number. They called me to tell me that there was an emergency at home and my son was badly injured! I rushed home (fortunately, the office was near the house), only to find that it was a very minor injury. I took him to a nearby hospital which had a separate section for foreigners. Unfortunately, that day it was very crowded, and it appeared that I would have to wait for a long time. I decided to take him to the Chinese section, one floor below. Since I did not know the language, I dialed my secretary for help. The doctor took one look at it for 5 seconds and instructed the nurse. She applied tincture on the bruise, put a bandage, and sent us home. It all took five minutes and cost 30 RMB (Rs 200). For the same treatment, the section for foreigners would have charged me $150 (~ 1,000 RMB or Rs 6,000). That's when I realised that, in many instances, foreigners paid doctors a huge premium for their knowledge of the English language and not necessarily for medical skills.

Superstitions and Beliefs

I once had an interesting discussion with a Chinese colleague in the office who was the head of a business. During the annual budgeting exercise, we had set the annual revenue target of his business unit as $404 million. He called me and asked me to reduce it by 5 million to $399 million, explaining to me that 4 is a very unlucky number in Chinese society. 404 had two fours, so it was a case of double trouble. I replied that changing it would be difficult, as it would mean increasing someone else's target by $5 million. After some discussion, he said, "well then, please assign a higher target of 405 or 406, but not 404". In my 25+ year finance career, it is the only instance of a salesperson asking for an increase in the revenue target.

The Chinese are very superstitious. It's about lucky charms, numbers, colours, stones, mountains, days of the week, animals, mascots, blah, blah, blah; stories abound for each of these. Companies also have their own lucky numbers and symbols. Even numbers are more auspicious than odd ones, so gifts are given in even numbers. Since the number 2 suggests germination and harmony, decorations in China are invariably set out in pairs, such as a pair of lions, a pair of candles, or pillows. The number 8 symbolises great luck, but its 'half-brother' 4 is a harbinger of bad luck since its pronunciation resembles that of the word 'death' (the Japanese have the same problem with 4, so they coined another word for it). In most buildings, there would be no floors numbered 4, 14, 24, 34, and so on. Our 66-storey apartment building actually had only 59 floors.

When buying gifts in China, one should avoid giving someone a clock. This is because, in that culture, giving a clock symbolises bidding farewell to someone on their deathbed – as if the days are numbered and time is limited. So, gifting someone a clock basically means you're sending them off to the great beyond. Animals also play a big role in Chinese superstitions. Dragons, used to represent men, are divine beings capable of bringing happiness and good fortune. Phoenixes, representing women, are also auspicious. While turtles are revered for their longevity in Chinese culture, they can also be a symbol of bad luck. For example, keeping a turtle as a pet may slow down your business[45].

Names are magic in the Chinese-speaking world, with people opting for names with an auspicious meaning. A good name, people say, can bring wealth, a brilliant career, and dazzling romance. According to a Chinese saying, a bad name is worse than being born to a bad life. In recent decades, in urban China, many of them acquire a Christian first name like Charles, Liz, or Victor. In keeping with the local culture, they do have a full Chinese name, but typically use a Christian name at work. Women have first names like Apple, April, May, and June. I used to tease them in the office that, as a society, they loved Q2 since April, May, June comprise the second quarter of the financial year.

New Year Legend

During Chinese New Year celebrations, unpleasant words like death, broken, killing, ghost, or sickness are avoided during conversations. Crying, washing, lending, and taking medicine are considered unlucky. The colour red is a national obsession and is associated with good luck - red sofas, red handkerchiefs, red paint, red pants - they truly 'see red' all the time. In the year of a person's Chinese zodiac sign, he/she is supposed to wear something red all year. So some part of their dress will most likely have the red colour, and if their dress doesn't have the colour in it, they will wear red innerwear. It made me realise why there were red lingerie on sale in so many shops.

The story behind the colour red is from Nian, the monster with a long head and sharp horns. It showed up every New Year's Eve to eat people and livestock in nearby villages. Therefore, on New Year's Eve, people would flee to remote mountains to avoid being harmed by the monster. An old man once visited the village and refused to hide in the mountains along with the villagers. He successfully scared away the monster by pasting red papers on doors, burning bamboo to make a loud cracking sound (precursor to firecrackers), lighting candles in the houses, and wearing red clothes. When the villagers came back, they were surprised to discover that the village had not been destroyed. After that, every New Year's Eve, people did as the old man instructed, and the monster Nian never showed up again. This tradition of celebrating the new year has remained, and Chinese New Year is referred to as Guo Nian, literally meaning "To overcome the Nian"[46].

The Chinese calendar years are represented by twelve zodiac animals - Rat, Ox, Tiger, Rabbit, Dragon, Snake, Horse, Sheep, Monkey, Rooster, Dog, and Pig. A person's personality, compatibility, and fortune **are** said to depend on their zodiac. People born in the Year of the Rat are instinctive, alert, brilliant businessmen, social, and adaptable. People born in the year of the Tiger are courageous, trustworthy, arrogant, and hasty[47]. There are many legends in Chinese folk culture as to why these twelve animals were chosen. The most widespread legend is that the Jade Emperor (the Emperor in Heaven in Chinese folklore) ordered that animals would be designated as calendar signs and the twelve that arrived first would be selected. Another belief is that the selection and sequence of the twelve animals **were** determined by the activity time of each animal. For example, the rat represents midnight because it becomes active at night from 11 pm to 1 am. Oxen begin to ruminate and start tilling the land between 1 and 3 am, the rooster becomes active between 5 and 7, and so on[48]. Two hours of each animal, times 12 of them, **make** a day of 24 hours.

Food

Let me start with a disappointing, piece of information for all lovers of Chinese food in India. In China, you do not get gobi manchurian (just as you can never get American chopsuey in America or play French Cricket in France). But the good part of travelling in China was that vegetarian food was easily available. We tend to perceive that it is hard to get vegetarian food in China. Not so true. In fact, it was easier than in Japan. Veganism, so widespread and one that has made global travel so much easier and pleasant now, barely existed then. Vegetables have always been an essential part of Chinese food and in restaurants; it is available and cooked tastily, the Chinese way. Whenever we travelled, at the time of making bookings, we would keep the travel agent informed that we **would** need vegetarian food. The agent's representative in the city we visited would ensure that we got rice and vegetables in every single meal. Even in restaurants in Shanghai, vegetarian food in the form of mock meat was available at many places, especially in Buddhist restaurants where they cook *Satvik* food and don't use meat, onion, or garlic. Cooking oils would also be vegetarian - or so we were told.

Chinese food can be quite exotic. They consume a lot of rice along with seafood of every type, creatures, insects, birds, and animals. They eat snake bile, crab glands, monkey brains, a bird's saliva, whole pigeons, locusts, scorpions, snails, reptiles, silkworms, frogs, starfish, grasshoppers, dog meat…….. As the expression goes, basically anything that has a mother and moves. They also use insects as food toppings. A disgusting sight used to be that of baby turtles, half the size of our palm, being sold on the streets. People would cook these turtles, fry them alive, scoop the flesh from their shells and add fillings to eat them. In the water city Zhou-zhuang (meaning Venice of the East), we saw turtles being fished out of the water and cracked open alive. During my stay, I could not taste even the things Indians usually eat (e.g., chicken), because a few years earlier, I turned a strict vegetarian, and so my status in China was that of a 'former' non-vegetarian.

A very expensive delicacy in China is Bird's nest soup. The Indonesian bird, Swiflet, nests in very high mountainous caves and when building its nest, it uses some twigs but mostly uses its saliva. Edible bird's nests are among the most expensive Chinese delicacies and tonics consumed by man. High-quality whole clean white nests can come from Sabah, Thailand, and Vietnam and can retail at well over two thousand dollars a pound. A bowl of soup can cost 600 RMB (Rs 4,000). For centuries, women in the Chinese royal families have been known to consume bird's nest to enhance beauty, skin, and complexion. Another expensive delicacy (about which we heard but never saw ourselves) used to be monkey brain, where the monkey would be brought alive to the customer's table in a restaurant, its head chopped, and the brain eaten. It is now banned in China and Hong Kong[49].

Food and hospitality habits include the host serving a large variety and quantity of food in every meal. The dining table has to be filled with about 10-12 dishes, intended to be far more than the guest can eat. Cooking and serving just enough is considered bad manners and makes the host feel that he/she did not make sufficient food for the guest, and thus having leftovers was considered a sign of good hospitality. On the part of the guest, finishing all the food served might also insult the host because it can imply that the host didn't provide enough food.

Religion

Writing about religion in China can be tricky. It starts with the most basic question: are they religious or atheist? Usually, this question arises about individuals, not about an entire nation. The answer itself can be vague. I looked up websites for statistics and didn't get anything useful. One site said 80% practice Taoism; another said 61% are strict atheists. While our perception is that those who are religious mostly follow Buddhism, both these websites said that Buddhism is followed by only about 6% of the people. I thought the best representation of their religious beliefs came from a study on this topic. I quote: "It's hard to say if the Chinese are religious. Many Chinese people who identify themselves as being atheist or non-religious frequently engage in what are normally considered religious activities (like going to the temple or burning incense).

In other words, it depends on what is meant by "religion". It seems that most Chinese define religion as belonging to an organised religious group, rather than consisting of practices such as praying in temples, and so they don't associate themselves with a specific religion. Yet, this does not prevent them from praying. Some Chinese say that they believe in Jesus Christ while denying that they are Christians[50]."

In ancient times, the Chinese were worshippers of nature - earth, heaven, sun, moon, stars, their ancestors, and other aspects of nature. They were not ritualistic even in times preceding the entry of Buddhism. In the sixth century BCE, drastic changes came in the field of religion through reformers Lao-Tse and Confucius who changed the Chinese religious outlook, taking it towards a more philosophical view of life[51]. Interestingly, Confucius, Lao-Tse, and Buddha were contemporaries of around the 6th century. Lao-Tse (or Old Master, born 604 BCE) is regarded as the first reformer and philosopher of ancient China. His teachings, Taoism (Tao meaning "the way"), were about a virtuous path and brought revolutionary changes in the field of religion in ancient China. The overall influence of Taoism seems limited.

The Chinese philosopher and teacher Confucius was born in 551 BCE and is considered one of the most important figures in world history. Confucianism was written by his disciples in the form of Analects, and its teachings in the areas of society and politics have created the foundation for how Chinese society should live life and engage in society. It focuses on the concept of *Ren*, i.e., compassion and love for others along with living peacefully and morally within the structures of society. While there is some resemblance to religion, since he talks about the afterlife and heaven, Confucius did not espouse belief in God. Few things have been more enduring or have had more impact on the Chinese than Confucianism (a few of his famous quotes are listed in Annexure 3).

The Three Gorges dam ship-lock system

A huge bus stop being moved 90 degrees.

English language sign-boards

Text in Image 1 "Slip and fall down carefully!"

Chapter 9

UNIQUELY CHINESE

Here are a few things that are fairly unique to the country. As I wrote it, I realised that, unlike say, Japan, some of it may not be completely unique, and may have similarities with India for example. But it is still a key characteristic of the country. What you will read in this chapter are the following assorted topics:

- The one-child policy
- Fake markets
- Re-creation for recreation (copying monuments)
- Moving a bus station 90 degrees
- Restriction on children playing online games
- Ancient Chinese medicine and
- Shanghainese men

The One-Child Policy

The one-child policy was introduced in 1979 and has avoided an estimated 400 million births[52]. Interestingly, just 30 years earlier, as part of his cultural revolution, Mao dictated that the population must be increased, encouraged its growth, and discouraged the use of contraception. Under the one-child policy, if a couple wanted a second child, they had to pay a fine, and the child could also be denied entitlements like free education.

The one-child policy meant that a typical family has 6 adults and one child - 4 grandparents, 2 parents, and a child. It's referred to as the 4-2-1 situation (sounds like a football formation). This 6:1 ratio meant that a lot of attention was given to the lone child, leading to the Little Emperor Syndrome. The child was pampered, growing up with a feeling of entitlement. Coupled with economic growth, the parents wanted to provide children with all that they themselves did not get, although that behaviour is true of many societies, especially immigrants into any country.

But the policy may have led to social and demographic issues – an ageing population with fewer younger generation people, thus reducing the workforce required to drive the economy. So, in 2016, the law was changed to allow couples to have two children. After the reform, China saw a short-lived boost in the fertility rate for 2016. Chinese women gave birth to 17.9 million babies in 2016, but the number of births declined by 3.5% to 17.2 million in 2017, and to 15.2 million in 2018. But, in general, people still appear to prefer having only one child due to the cost of childcare. Chinese couples were also polled and stated that they would rather invest in one child, as opposed to two children. In May 2018, it was reported that Chinese authorities were in the process of ending their population control policies. In May 2021, the Chinese government announced it would scrap the two-child policy in favour of a three-child policy, allowing couples to have three children to mitigate the country's falling birth rates[53].

Here's some humour about learning Mandarin in school. While teaching the language, children are taught words for close relatives such as brother, sister, uncle, aunt, and cousin. My 11-year-old son, who already carried the burden of unlearning Japanese and learning Mandarin, found it annoying that he had to learn words that barely get used in society. Due to the one-child policy, people anyway did not have uncles, aunts, or siblings.

After learning Japanese in Japan, he had to learn Mandarin. So there was another round of unlearning & learning. During the early days of learning Mandarin, in the class, out of habit, he used a Japanese word. The teacher was quite upset. She warned him not to repeat the mistake. Japan and China have the same relationship as, say, India and Pakistan. No great love **exists** between the countries. So, using Japanese was more than just a mistake.

Male Child Weakness

My 18-year-old nephew was visiting us from Mumbai. My wife planned our first trip to Beijing at this time. I could not join them, so it was a team of a mother, two sons, and a nephew – i.e., three boys, aged between 12 and 18. During the trip, much to her surprise, many women would stop to see "a woman who had three boys"! No one in their society had this privilege. They would ask her, "You have 3 boys, wow". It was like saying, "Oh, you blessed one". She did not know enough Mandarin, and in some cases did not bother, to clarify that all three boys were not her children. One lady, in fact, requested taking a photograph with her and the boys. What an unlikely reason for celebrity status. My younger son knew some Mandarin and suggested taunting them, that another (fourth) boy was at home, but was, of course, silenced by my wife.

For centuries, the Chinese have had a weakness for boys and, perhaps, provided them favourable treatment in education and nourishment. The ratio of men to women in China is approximately 113:100[54], with Azerbaijan having the weakest ratio in the world – 117:100. In India, it's 108:100. Their reason for male preference is the same as the one cited in India - seeking descendants to carry on the "vansh" (family lineage) and having more earning members at home. In recent decades, their male child weakness must also be viewed in the context of the one-child policy.

Is the Gender Ratio Supposed to be 50:50?

Interestingly, the World Health Organisation (WHO) estimates that the 'expected' sex ratio at birth for most countries would be 105 males per 100 female births. Why not 50:50? A study showed that the sex ratio at conception is equal: there is no difference in the number of males and females conceived. For births to be consistently male-biased, there must be gender differences in the probability of miscarriage through pregnancy. The study found that although the probability of miscarriage varies between genders across the course of pregnancy, female mortality is slightly higher than male mortality over the full period[55]. Hence, there is a slight bias in the male-female ratio.

While on the topic of gender ratio, here's a billboard advertisement I saw many years back in an Indian magazine. Aimed at increasing awareness of gender imbalance and the risk of men not finding brides, the ad was in the form of a wedding invitation card. It read:

"Satish and Deepak Wed Neha"

It was meant to scare readers that gender imbalance would soon lead to this state of affairs. Very creative and telling ad, I thought.

Fake Markets

Ah, the ubiquitous fake markets. When moving into a new city, one quickly takes to its local attractions, especially if it's about shopping. We have all been familiar with fake products from Hong Kong for decades and more recently from China. Near our house, there were two full buildings housing hundreds of small shops. In the fake markets, one could get electronics, textiles, watches, cosmetics, perfumes, phones... you name it – "Ma, baap ke alava" (everything except mother and father) types. Fake versions of Burberry, Louis Vuitton, Gucci, Prada et al. If the original product had extra features like special packing or a small booklet explaining the product features and finery, the duplicate will have that too, reproduced in exactly the same way. 'Rolex' watches were available on the streets for $3 and in shops for $30 and $300. One of the fake markets in Shanghai occupied a few floors below the city's Science and Technology museum.

Shopping in these markets was a fun experience with lots of negotiation and a hard bargain. A T-shirt would be quoted at RMB 250 (~Rs 3,000 or $40). Our counter-offer would be 1/10th that price. Due to language barrier, bargaining between foreigners and shopkeepers happened by typing quotes and counter-offers on a calculator. After a lot of back and forth, the final price would be, say, 30 RMB (1/8th of the amount first quoted). One had to do the usual drama of walking away from the store and returning. There were nuances even to this. The negotiations and final price depended on nationality. As a local person once explained to us, there were three price ranges in which goods were sold. The highest charge would be to Westerners who converted prices to $s and found it cheap even at high prices. With Asians, the mathematical factor would change from division to multiplication, i.e., a European would divide the cost by say 7, whereas an Indian would multiply by 11. So, they would offer a lower price to Asians who bargained harder, paying perhaps half of what the Westerners paid. The third level of pricing, i.e., the lowest price, was for the local Chinese, because they knew the real price.

A combination of fake goods and bargained prices would mean that you can't take the quality and brand too seriously. But it is still in our nature to do it. At a shop near our house, when shopping for handbags, my wife liked a particular bag and looked all over it to find out which brand it was. Not finding any brand label, she asked the shopkeeper, "What brand is it?" He said, "Lady, whatever brand you want, you say, I put" ☺. He had the brand logos of all brands in a drawer and would simply pick the one the customer asked for and stick it on the bag.

Fabric Markets

Similar to Indians, they are very ingenious. Shanghai's massive and famous fabric market is a good example. We used to go there and look for pants, shirts, and suits – both male and female. They would stitch the material within a few days or even in 24 hours if required. The tailors excelled at replicating fashion clothing of the best international brands. After reading about this market, my niece from the U.S took a cutting of a stylish dress design from a fashion magazine, sent it to my wife, and asked for it to be tailored similarly. Just by seeing the picture, the tailor reproduced the design, down to the lowest detail, and stunningly close to the original. She really liked the end product and was amazed at how well it was done. If they can please a young American girl on customised fashion, you have to salute their skill.

Ancient Medicine

There appear to be similarities in the principles of ancient Indian and Chinese medicine. Systems of ancient medicine in both India and China go beyond just the symptom and consider the relationship of the different parts of the body in analysing an illness. These systems work on the basis that the human body and nature are interconnected, and illness occurs in the process of the body's interaction with nature. Here are a few assorted aspects of Chinese medicine and their equivalents in the Indian medical system.

Nadas, Prana

As per Chinese medicine, meridians in the body act as channels and carry energy into every tissue of the body. This appears similar to Nadas ("Nad") in yoga, meaning channel or movement. If meridians or Nada are the energy channels, Qi (pronounced chi), which is similar to Prana in yoga sutra, is believed to be the main energy force behind all things on earth. The principle in both systems is that when energy flow is clear and unblocked, people have good health. Blocking of flows due to various factors such as food and lifestyle creates health problems, and practices such as Yoga and Qi help correct the imbalance. Acupuncture and acupressure, as well as asanas in yoga, play the role of rebalancing energy. They unblock the build-up of imbalances and bring the body's Qi or Prana to flow back to normal, returning to its natural and healthy state.

Isn't it amazing that two civilisations, working independently some 3,000 years ago, on something as complex as the human body, discovered the same basic principle of how the body and illness work and identified energy flow as one of the root causes of good health or illness? An equally interesting facts is that the world's most popular form of medicine, Allopathy, after years of intense and high-quality research, does not recognise this element of energy channels in the human body as relevant to diagnosis and treatment (I am only stating a fact, not criticising Allopathy).

Nadi or pulse reading is an important form of diagnosis of illness in Tibetan medicine, similar to the Indian medical systems of Siddha Vaidya and Ayurveda. Apparently, in Tibetan medicine, doctors can diagnose 40 different forms of illness just by reading the pulse. I have experimented with Tibetan medicine and actually experienced this when the doctor called out an ailment that I had not even mentioned to him. I was under treatment for a lung problem with a Tibetan doctor in Bangalore. On one occasion when I went in for consultation, he studied my pulse and asked me if I have lower-back pain. I did. I was quite amazed because I never mentioned it to him that day or had it come up in prior conversations.

Pulse reading reminds me of a joke from many Indian movies of the 60s and 70s. A married woman would suddenly faint. The doctor would be summoned home. He/she would read her pulse, diagnose and declare that the woman was pregnant. The hilarious part would be that later, when the woman very shyly informs her husband of the pregnancy, the guy will be joyous but also surprised about the news – saying "Oh, really." "Excuse me, Mr Husband, you did not know"?

Panchabhuta

The Chinese too believe in Panchabhutas, i.e., the 5 life force elements that exist in the universe in both organic and inorganic things[56] and symbolise energy, movement, and change. Of the 5 elements in the Indian system, 3 are common with the Chinese system and 2 are different.

Indian Panchabhutas: Water, Earth, Fire, Air, Sky (Akash)

Chinese Panchabhutas: Water, Earth, Fire, Wood, Metal

Acupuncture

The acupuncture form of medicine uses needles and fire to cure an illness - both being essential and correlated. During acupuncture, the needles stimulate the sensory neurons which help direct the flow of hormones and nervous system signals through the body. The pricks of needles on acupuncture points adjust the organic functions and clear the energy channels of the obstruction in our body which stimulates blood flow[57]. You may have observed a recent instance in world sports of the use of the Acupuncture technique called Cupping. It's a technique done to reduce soreness and heal overworked muscles. During the 2016 Rio Olympics, the legendary athlete and swimmer Michael Phelps is said to have used this form of treatment and had purple colour cup marks on his back while entering the swimming pool.

My Reflexology Experience

Shanghai had numerous massage parlours that provided body massage and foot reflexology (some of these places were apparently shady ones, masquerading as 'massage' parlours, providing the body more than a massage). The foot reflexology centre that we frequented near our house was called Blind Massage Centre since it was staffed by fully or partially blind people - a nice way of providing employment to the disabled. I had an interesting experience once while having a foot massage done. When the masseur pressed a certain area of my foot, I felt a sharp pain and immediately reacted with an Aah. Pointing to her lungs, the blind masseuses enquired if I had a breathing problem! Amazing, because I did, in fact, have a problem with my lungs. It proved to me, beyond doubt, the science of acupressure and reflexology, which works on the theory that each pressure point in the feet corresponds to an organ or part of the body.

Raga Trivia

Many of the restaurants played music, mildly (unlike in India, where it is invariably loud and tends to drown one of the main purposes of visiting a restaurant - conversations). I, and some of my friends, observed some familiarity between the music that was being played and Indian classical music. We then figured out that the equivalent of raga Mohanam (Carnatic music) and its counterpart, raag Bhoop/Bhopali (Hindustani music) is one a popular musical scale in China. I later read that this tune is also popular in East Asian and South-East Asian music, including Japan.

Re-Creation for Recreation

For aesthetics and tourism, the local Governments recreated replicas of many world-famous travel destinations. Here are a few examples of the many miniature copies of landmarks around the globe built in China:

1. Hangzhou city, which holds a stunning replica of parts of Paris, including the Eiffel Tower, the Arc de Triomphe, and classic paintings.

2. Hallstatt Village in Guangdon: Hallstatt is a quaint Austrian village, a very popular tourist destination in recent years. Building its carbon copy cost $940 million.

3. The Tower Bridge of London in Suzhou.

4. Colosseum in Macau (see picture): Instead of building the replica of the Colosseum in Rome as an amphitheatre, just like its original counterpart, the Chinese made the Colosseum in Macau as a shopping mall in the city's Fisherman's Wharf. Who wouldn't want to shop at one of history's greatest monuments?

They have also built versions of China's own Great Wall in different places[58].

Moving a Bus Station 90 Degrees

Engineers in a Chinese city have moved a bus terminal to a new location by pushing the entire five-storey building across the ground. The building is equivalent to four Eiffel Towers in weight and was moved in the space of 40 days to give way to bullet trains. To relocate the massive 30,000-tonne structure whole, workers put hundreds of hydraulic jacks under it and laid rolling tracks for it to slide along.

A transport plan to facilitate a high-speed railway project in the city required the terminal to move to a nearby street. After rounds of consultations, the city's authorities decided to push the entire building from one street to another. The ambitious move would require the building to make a 90-degree turn horizontally using one side of it as the centre point (see picture).

Moving such a heavy and large building quickly is an unprecedented challenge. They dug the ground, put railings along the ground in the fan-shaped area, and lifted the building off the ground and put 532 hydraulic jacks underneath. The bus terminal was pushed forwards for 10 to 20 metres (32.8 to 65.6 feet) a day[59].

Shanghainese Men

Let me wrap up this chapter by talking about Shanghainese men. They, it appears, make great husbands and are considered special and quite different from men from other parts of China. They don't just shop, wash, and cook but famously do so without complaint. The attraction of Shanghai men seems to be their mild temperament and the way they respect their brides[60]. In humour, they are portrayed as a henpecked husband in movies, TV, or theatre. However, they also carry a reputation in business circles for being among the best negotiators.

Restriction on Online Games

To combat internet addiction, for years, the Chinese authorities have implemented measures that parents across the world will appreciate - seeking to control how much time kids can spend playing games online. In 2019, authorities restricted minors to playing 90 minutes a day on weekdays and banned them from playing between 10 p.m. and 8 a.m. In 2021, they issued even stricter regulations: Minors were allowed to play online games for only an hour a day and only on Fridays, weekends, and public holidays.

In November — more than a year after the stricter game controls were introduced — a government-affiliated industry group, Game Industry Group Committee, issued a report declaring that the gaming addiction problem among minors was "basically resolved." even as the three-hour weekly limit for Friday, Saturday, and Sunday stayed in place. Overall, the Group's report said, more than 75% of minors in China played online games for less than three hours a week. Many parents have praised the restrictions, even as their children threw tantrums. Social media and games companies set up or strengthened "Youth Mode" settings on their apps meant to protect minors. They include features that limit use, control payments, and display age-appropriate content. For some popular games, real-name registration and even facial recognition gateways have been implemented to prevent workarounds[61].

Chapter 10

BUSINESS CUSTOMS AND ETIQUETTE – A BRIEF LOOK

In business, as elsewhere in Asia, relationships are very important, and the conduct and quantum of business depend on relationships. The business etiquette is such as to build what the Chinese call Guanxi (gwan shee), i.e., social or business connections based on mutual interest and benefit. It is not about making fair-weather friends. Relationships must be maintained through regular contact. New business relationships will begin with many casual or dinner meetings before they get down to the actual business discussions. Many business deals are sealed outside of working hours over informal meetings and dinner. The principle behind Guanxi is that once trust is generated, business will invariably follow. A lot of business is done based on trust.

This tradition is not new to Indians. The high-value diamond business in Surat, which has worked for over a hundred years, is based on trust. Diamonds are handed over to angadias or couriers without even a contract, who move diamonds worth millions, based on trust and word. Backing the system is community relationships where communities in villages and towns, comprising family members, all engaging in the same business, create a certain bonding and mutual personal responsibility in performance at work. Any breach of a relationship will get noticed by the entire community and have an immediate impact on the social lives of those involved.

As we read about the Japanese, keeping "face" is very important in Chinese business. People hate losing face and being embarrassed for any reason. There's a saying in the Chinese language that goes 人要┌┌要皮, which translates to mean "Men can't live without face, trees can't live without bark". If you are in business, you'll likely be introduced to potent Chinese rice wine known as baijiu and are expected to give and participate in toasts throughout the evening. Abstaining from the consumption of alcohol is possible but will likely require a lot of willpower and a little bit of relationship capital. It's ingrained in Chinese business culture to believe that you never really know a person until you've been drunk with them[62].

The credibility of information released by the government has been a source of much concern in the global business community. I happened to meet a U.S MNC employee who has worked with both India and China and asked how he compared them. He said that "In China, if you want to understand the business or economic environment and speak to, say, four officials in different government departments and government companies, the information they share would be fairly similar and consistent. It may or may not be fully accurate. On the one hand, the consistency and similarity of the opinion would seem like an advantage because if true, it would make decision-making easier. But the risk perhaps stems from the fact that they are perhaps telling you what they want you to believe. He said that the Indian business scenario is different. Four different people can give you varied and contradictory views on the same topic and back it up with data. Because people give you their personal view or the view of that particular organisation, after hearing diverse voices, it is now up to us to form our own judgement and conclusion". Interesting observation and contrast.

Quality

Are the Chinese quality-conscious? There is a clear dichotomy here because, on the one hand, they have huge exports, but at the same time, "Made in China" is also associated with poor durability. There is a cartoon on social media where the famous Mr. Bean quipped – "Weekends must be made in China - they don't last long[63]"!

But, without quality, the country could not have become a global manufacturing supplier those exports trillions of dollars of goods that the rest of the world is comfortable consuming. Global companies from all over the world have been buying from them for years. We all use phones, computers, fashion products made there which have been of good quality. The reason for the apparent dichotomy could be that there is the manufacture of both high-quality and cheaper goods.

Chapter 11

CHEXIT

Two years after we arrived, it was time for our family to exit China and return home. Living in a country changes one's perceptions of it, and this was true in our case. We could move freely within the country, and people felt safe living there. We saw for ourselves the extraordinary transformation and development in the country, where 800 million people were lifted above the poverty line in a span of just 25 years.

The country is often compared with India because it is Asian and because of the size of the population. We got a much better appreciation of the similarities and differences in societal culture and customs. Unfortunately, like other foreigners there, due to language barriers, we had very little opportunity to socialise with the local Chinese people, unlike in India where foreigners interact with the locals socially.

An office colleague, a Chinese person, once shared an observation after his trip to India about Indians: apparently, Indians smile much more. Another person who visited India made a similar observation. They said that wherever they went, they found a lot of vibrancy in the country and people, including poor children on the street who smiled more. They were pleasantly surprised by this.

The biggest headline news about China in recent decades is its economic growth. I had a dilemma on deciding whether to include this topic in the book. There are two ways to look at it. One, that the topic of the economy would be very out-of-place in a storybook like this one and be boring to many. Two, it is such a big feature of China that completely avoiding it does not make sense. So I decided to write very briefly on it and have presented it in Annexure 1, so that people interested in it can read it.

Chapter 12

FLYING BACK TO THE NEST

And so, a tale-of-three-cities came to an end. We lived for short stints of two years or less in each of them and moved in quick succession. Three countries, four moves, five years - that's how it rhymes.

A satirical discussion of our family's quick relocation between countries came from a very unexpected source – a sportsman. When we were new to Shanghai, a few international cricketers came to play a *Shanghai 6s* tournament. We had gone to watch it, and my sons approached a famous retired Australian cricketer for an autograph. He was sitting alone in a tent and was friendly and chatted with them:

Cricketer (C): Have you been living here for many years?

The boys (B): No, we came here just 2 months back.

C: You came here from India? Where in India?

B: No. We moved here from Tokyo.

C: Oh, so you went from India to Tokyo & came here.

B: No. We went from Bangalore to Singapore, then to Tokyo, and are now here in Shanghai.

C: Does your father work for IBM?

Oh, what a question! Even he knew that many IBMers on international assignments moved countries frequently. I had only proved right the joke among employees that maybe IBM should stand for *I'm Being Moved.*

Upon our return, our friends in India were curious to know how our sons adapted to the many changes in education. It was undoubtedly very tough. My older son changed five schools in seven years, and the younger one seven schools in seven years (including a mid-year change)!! They had to continuously un-learn and re-learn, make several adjustments, make and give up friends and teachers at a rapid pace and transitioned from learning Kannada to Japanese and Mandarin. They, naturally, protested each time but accepted and moved on. Since their ages during our overseas stay ranged from 8 to 16, they could experience different countries and participate in a multi-language, multi-cultural environment at a stage of life when their opinions were being formed and shaped. Post-event, till this date, the boys (now men) feel the same way – an experience that was very difficult but worth it. I may not be too far off the mark if I said that those few years were among the best for the family. The challenges, the global exposure, the uncertainties and varying cultures have left behind many memories that we regularly recall even today.

Our friends asked us to rank our preference of the three countries. Our order of liking was Japan, China, and Singapore. Many were surprised that clean, green, and efficient Singapore was ranked third. Such is the power of history and of civilisation, of nations and cultures. There was so much to travel, observe, relate to, compare, question, make fun of, and enjoy in the two countries. It is hard for a very small and young Singapore to offer and unfair on our part to expect out of it.

Similar to India, the three countries we lived in are all relationship-based societies in personal life and in the culture of doing business. All have tough, grinding school and education environments for locals. They have very tight immigration laws, contributing perhaps to their being much safer places to live in compared with many other parts of the world. In Japan, the government rewarded couples with money for having a baby whereas, in China, citizens were fined for having a second baby. The Japanese have complete freedom of speech but by culture don't speak openly. The Chinese would like to speak more freely in public. Indians, of course, make up for all that by thinking and speaking so freely that each of us has at least 1.7 opinions on every topic on the planet – be it on our economy, quantum physics, how much nuclear arsenal each country should have, what should be the right strategy in Rugby (a game we don't play) and so on! Singapore and China are tightly government controlled, with an ability to think far on economic matters. Japan, like India, is democracy at its best.

The Flight Back To India

We were at the Singapore airport for the last, Singapore-Bengaluru leg of our journey. Our flight was delayed by more than an hour. As we boarded, the hostess announced that the "delay is due to the late arrival of the incoming flight". Extremely useful information. Well, at least better than the announcement at the Beijing airport that "delay is due to the airline". (Btw, generally speaking, I find that during the flight, airlines share funny or fairly useless information. The pilot will make announcements like "The outside temperature is minus 35 degrees, but for your comfort, we have kept the cabin at 24 degrees". Wow. You mean the cabin too could have been kept at minus 35 or was there an option to keep the windows open and let passengers enjoy the outside temperature?. They also announce during landing that the "tail wind is 60 km per hour and visibility 4 kms". Is 4km good or bad. Am I supposed to feel safe or get scared? How does it matter to the passenger?)

The flight back from Singapore was smooth, but the family's thoughts turbulent, flying faster than the aircraft we were in, swinging from nostalgia to expectation of the future, from challenging times and trivia to some fond memories that we carry to this day. It seemed like just the other day when I was offered a role outside India and here I was heading back home.

The air hostess informed the passengers that we were about to touch down at Bangalore. No matter what your age, there is a child-like joy in returning home, and I felt that. A few minutes later, the hostess announced that the outside temperature was 25 degrees Celsius. Where else in this planet will you get such lovely weather at 11 am in June.......

It had to be **B e n g a l u r u**!

ANNEXURES

ANNEXURE 1:
CHINA'S ECONOMIC GROWTH STORY

China's growth to economic superpower status in just a few decades is unprecedented in the history of economic development. Around 1980, it was a poor country with a GDP of $200 billion and a population of one billion. By 2016, the GDP grew a whopping 55 times to $11.2 trillion! It has helped lift ~800 million people out of poverty.

In 1978, Mao's successor, Deng Xiaoping, started the historic transformation to the China of today. Several factors led to such success, including having great visionary leaders, a very powerful government, and a quest for continuous growth. Planning and execution of mega ideas and projects were superb. They made decisions that would appear unthinkable for a communist country - allowing private enterprise and a free market that would go on to create wealth for the country and its citizens. To back their focus on manufacturing, they made massive investments in infrastructure, created economic/export zones, maintained flexible government policies, and made their exports competitive. China is also blessed with very large natural resource deposits like coal, oil and gas, gold, and rare earth metals.

Decision-making by the government was quick, and people showed high adaptability in responding to change. These attributes remain true to date. Let me quote from an old article in the New York Times[64]: "When Apple needed to quickly re-engineer its iPhone screens, it inevitably turned to Chinese factories because none in the U.S. could meet the necessary turn-around time. New screens began arriving at the plant at midnight. A foreman immediately roused 8,000 workers inside the company's dormitories. Each employee was given a biscuit and a cup of tea, guided to a workstation and within half an hour started a 12-hour shift fitting glass screens into bevelled frames. Within 96 hours, the plant was producing over 10,000 iPhones a day."

Early in the '80s and '90s, the government regularly showcased its strengths as a large and attractive market for foreign companies, helping bring in technology and massive investments. Developing Shenzhen into an industrial town, building large airports and a financial street in Beijing are examples of showcasing capability. Even their political structure evolved to facilitate this rapid transformation. States and provinces were given wide powers to invest and attract foreign investment, and contrary to the past, they moved from a centralised to a more decentralised approach, allowing the states/provinces to make important and successful decisions.

The structure of banks must have contributed to their success too. The country's money is with just four nationally-owned banks. The stupendous job growth brought in much higher income to the people. Like Indians, the Chinese are thrifty which they put into the banks. With all business and personal money going into just four banks, they could invest more easily in infrastructure, factories, and businesses.

A lot of credit should go to its people who worked very hard, helping achieve the country's goals. In return, they were rewarded with jobs, better living, and opportunities for private wealth creation. The Chinese have a high work ethic and are generally compliant to processes or rules.

The benefit of an entire country working towards one goal is huge. China's 1.4 billion people are a homogeneous society in terms of language and culture, making it easier to bring people together for a purpose.

A measure of the greater efficiency of China is in the table below. This data on agriculture shows that with only 60% of India's cultivated land area, China produces more than 2 times more food.

Agriculture[65]	India	China
Land under cultivation (million km2)	1.7	1.2
Total land being used for agricultural cultivation	53%	13%
Food grain output (million tonnes) (2015-16)	250	570

ANNEXURE 2:
NATURAL DISASTERS IN CHINA

Wars and natural disasters claiming an extraordinary number of lives have been a dominant part of history in the last about 2000 years. Yet, in reading about China, the number of such events and lives lost is saddening. Apparently, it has had 6 of the top 10 floods and landslides of all time, 3 of the top 10 most fatal earthquakes, and 6 of the top 10 most deadly famines.

Floods, drought, war, rebellion in China

	Event	Period	Estimated death in million	Comments
1	Nian Rebellion, Taiping Rebellion and drought	1850-1873	10-30	Primarily caused by famine, lower life expectancy and plague in the case of the Nian rebellion
2	Northern Chinese Famine	1876–79	9.5-13	
3	Famine in northern Anhui, northern Jiangsu	1906-07	20-25	
4	Great Chinese famine	1959-61	17-45	
5	Yellow river floods	1887	0.9	
6	Yantze huai river floods	1931	2.0	Drowning and lack of food

	Event	Period	Estimated death in million	Comments
7	Nanjing massacre - Sino-Japanese war	1937	0.1 -0.2	
8	An Lushan rebellion	755-763	13	It was a revolt against the Tang dynasty of Imperial China
9	The Taiping rebellion	1850-1864	20	It was a civil war in China between the Manchu-led Qing dynasty and the Hakka-led Taiping Heavenly Kingdom.
10	Shaanxi earthquake	1556	0.8	100,000 of these were caused by earthquake, while over 700,000 migrated and died from famine and plagues
11	Dungan revolt	1862-1877	20	Comprised two waves of uprising which were eventually suppressed by Qing forces

ANNEXURE 3:

QUOTES BY *CONFUCIUS* [66] [67]

Everything has its beauty, but not everyone sees it.

It does not matter how slowly you go so long as you do not stop.

Our greatest glory is not in never falling, but in rising every time we fall.

I want you to be everything that's you, deep at the centre of your being.

I hear and I forget. I see and I remember. I do and I understand.

Choose a job you love, and you will never have to work a day in your life.

Wheresoever you go, go with all your heart.

Real knowledge is to know the extent of one's ignorance.

The superior man acts before he speaks, and afterwards speaks according to his action.

To know what you know and what you do not know, that is true knowledge.

To be wronged is nothing unless you continue to remember it.

When anger rises, think of the consequences.

ANNEXURE 4: JAPANESE WORDS

For those interested in it, here are a few Japanese words and their meaning.

English	Japanese
Hello	Konnichiwa
Thank you	Arigato Guzaimasu
I understand	Wakarimashta
I don't understand	Rikaidekinai
Is it so?	Sodesu ka
Yes, I know	Sodesu ne
You are welcome	Do Itashimshite
Are you ok? /I am ok	Daijobudesuka
How are you	Genkidesu ka
I am fine	Genkidesuka (or watashi wa genkidesu)
Good Morning	Ohayo Gozaimasu
Good afternoon	Konnichiwa
Name	Namae
Water	Mizu
Excellent	Subarashi
Right	Migi
Left	Hidari
Straight	Masugu
Near	Chikaku
Bye	Sayonara
Zero to 10	Zero, Ichi, Ni, San, Yon, Go, Rokku, Sichi (or nana), Hachi, Kyu, Jyu

REFERENCES

1. https://www.gotokyo.org/en/destinations/southern-tokyo/roppongi/index.html#:~:text
2. Japan times.co.jp
3. https://mai-ko.com/travel/culture-in-japan/japanese-culture-1/#:~:text
4. https://mai-ko.com/travel/culture-in-japan/japanese-culture-1/#:~:text
5. https://spice.fsi.stanford.edu/docs/geography_of_japan
6. https://asia.nikkei.com/Spotlight/Society/Japan-population-to-fall-below-100m-by-2056-new-estimate
7. https://culturalatlas.sbs.com.au/japanese-culture/japanese-culture-religion
8. https://culturalatlas.sbs.com.au/japanese-culture/japanese-culture-religion
9. https://spiritofjapantours.com/sacred-fire-goma-ceremony/
10. https://www.japan-guide.com/e/e3900.html
11. https://www.discoverkyoto.com/places-go/sanjusangen-do/
12. https://en.wikipedia.org/wiki/Sanjūsangen-dō
13. https://www.busuu.com/en/japanese/alphabet
14. https://www.theknot.com/content/japanese-wedding-traditions
15. https://www.france24.com/en/20191206-parasite-singles-why-young-japanese-aren-t-getting-married
16. https://www.japanesestudies.org.uk/discussionpapers/ 2006/Tran.html
17. https://www.japantimes.co.jp/community/2023/04/10/issues/take-make-long-term-relationship-great-japan/
18. https://dailypost.ng/2023/05/02/countries-with-highest-rates-of-divorce-revealed-see-list/#:~:text
19. https://www.theguardian.com/news/2007/oct/18/internationalnews

20. https://www.theguardian.com/news/2007/oct/18/internationalnews
21. https://www.nippon.com/en/currents/d00362/
22. https://en.wikipedia.org/wiki/List_of_the_heaviest_sumo_wrestlers
23. https://www.insidejapantours.com/blog/2014/09/16/11-amazing-things-you-probably-never-knew-about-sumo-wrestling/
24. https://www.justonecookbook.com/chanko-nabe-sumo-stew/
25. https://livinginjapan.net/2019/05/00242/
26. https://www.joincake.com/blog/kotsuage/
27. https://www.pilotguides.com/articles/japanese-tea-ceremony/
28. https://mai-ko.com/travel/culture-in-japan/tea-ceremony/what-is-the-relationship-between-zen-and-tea-ceremony/
29. https://education.nationalgeographic.org/resource/tohoku-earthquake-and-tsunami/
30. Source: CNN
31. https://opexlearning.com/resources/japan-earthquake-2011-queueing/8321/
32. https://apts.jp/tokyo-life/the-cost-of-keeping-a-cat-or-a-dog-in-japan/
33. https://mai-ko.com/travel/culture-in-japan/manners-in-japan/business-etiquette-in-japan/
34. https://www.americanexpress.com/en-us/business/trends-and-insights/articles/doing-business-in-japan-10-etiquette-rules-you-should-know/
35. https://livejapan.com/en/in-tokyo/in-pref-tokyo/in-tokyo_train_station/article-a0002470/
36. https://en.wikipedia.org/wiki/Terracotta_Army
37. https://www.history.com/news/first-earliest-human-civilizations#:~:text
38. https://china.usc.edu/sites/default/files/forums/Chinese%20Inventions.pdf
39. https://data.worldbank.org/indicator/SL.TLF.CACT.FE.ZS?locations=CN
40. https://www.bbc.co.uk/languages/chinese/real_chinese/mini_guides/char.
41. https://www.todaytranslations.com/about/language-history/chinese-language history/#:~:text

42. asia-knowledge.tki.org.nz
43. https://www.boredpanda.com/funny-chinese-translation-fails/?utm_source=google&utm_medium=organic&utm_campaign=organic
44. https://www.china-mike.com/facts-about-china/chinese-superstitions/
45. https://www.chinahighlights.com/travelguide/festivals/chinese-new-year-legends.htm#google_vignette
46. traditions.cultural-china.com
47. chinatravelguide.com
48. flavourfortunes.com
49. chinasource.org
50. travelchinaguide.com
51. https://www.britannica.com/story/the-effects-of-chinas-one-child-policy#
52. https://en.wikipedia.org/wiki/Two-child_policy#:~:text=According%20to%20The%20Economist%2C%20the,in%20fertility%20rate%20for%202016.
53. https://ourworldindata.org/gender-ratio
54. https://ourworldindata.org/gender-ratio
55. ncbi.nlm.nih.gov
56. travelchinaguide.com
57. *https://www.esquiremag.ph/the-good-life/pursuits/5-chinese-knockoffs-of-world-famous-travel-destinations-a1593-20161217-lfrm; By Hannah lazatin*
58. https://www.dailymail.co.uk/news/article-6886029/Chinese-engineers-30-000-tonne-bus-terminal-40-days.html
59. https://www.globaltimes.cn/content/699247.shtml
60. https://apnews.com/article/gaming-business-children. China keeping 1 hour daily limit on kids' online games
61. https://www.china-briefing.com/news/doing-business-china-etiquette-culture-travel/
62. https://www.pinterest.com/pin/i-think-the-weekends-are-made-in-china-they-dont-last-long--518125132126491700/
63. https://opencanada.org/the-secret-of-chinas-success/
64. indiaspend.com
65. confuciusquotes.com and brainyquotes.com
66. confuciusquotes.com and brainyquotes.com

References relating to Annexure 2

1 - 4	https://en.wikipedia.org/wiki/List_of_famines_in_China
5	https://en.wikipedia.org/wiki/List_of_disasters_in_China_by_death_toll
6	https://en.wikipedia.org/wiki/1931_China_floods
7	https://en.wikipedia.org/wiki/List_of_disasters_in_China_by_death_toll
8	https://historycollection.com/20-wars-in-history-that-left-behind-devastating-death-tolls/14/
9	https://en.wikipedia.org/wiki/Taiping_Rebellion#
10	https://en.wikipedia.org/wiki/1556_Shaanxi_earthquake#
11	https://en.wikipedia.org/wiki/Dungan_Revolt_(1862–1877)

Credits relating to English language sign-boards

Image credits (in order of pictures): tinypic.com, Chris Radley, offbeatchina.com, offbeatchina.com, imgur.com, dingadingdang

OTHER BOOKS PUBLISHED BY THE AUTHOR

ABOUT THE AUTHOR

Ramanan Ravikumar is a Chartered Accountant and former Chief Financial Officer (CFO) of IBM India/ South Asia. He has lived and worked in four countries, providing him with multicultural exposure. He loves to listen to music (both classical and film music), read books of different genre, watch sports, and is fascinated by gravity, genetics, and bird migration. He lives with his wife in Bengaluru, and has two sons.